SpringerBriefs in Education

We are delighted to announce SpringerBriefs in Education, an innovative product type that combines elements of both journals and books. Briefs present concise summaries of cutting-edge research and practical applications in education. Featuring compact volumes of 50 to 125 pages, the SpringerBriefs in Education allow authors to present their ideas and readers to absorb them with a minimal time investment. Briefs are published as part of Springer's eBook Collection. In addition, Briefs are available for individual print and electronic purchase.

SpringerBriefs in Education cover a broad range of educational fields such as: Science Education, Higher Education, Educational Psychology, Assessment & Evaluation, Language Education, Mathematics Education, Educational Technology, Medical Education and Educational Policy.

SpringerBriefs typically offer an outlet for:

- An introduction to a (sub)field in education summarizing and giving an overview of theories, issues, core concepts and/or key literature in a particular field
- A timely report of state-of-the art analytical techniques and instruments in the field of educational research
- A presentation of core educational concepts
- An overview of a testing and evaluation method
- A snapshot of a hot or emerging topic or policy change
- An in-depth case study
- A literature review
- A report/review study of a survey
- An elaborated thesis

Both solicited and unsolicited manuscripts are considered for publication in the SpringerBriefs in Education series. Potential authors are warmly invited to complete and submit the Briefs Author Proposal form. All projects will be submitted to editorial review by editorial advisors.

SpringerBriefs are characterized by expedited production schedules with the aim for publication 8 to 12 weeks after acceptance and fast, global electronic dissemination through our online platform SpringerLink. The standard concise author contracts guarantee that:

- an individual ISBN is assigned to each manuscript
- each manuscript is copyrighted in the name of the author
- the author retains the right to post the pre-publication version on his/her website or that of his/her institution

More information about this series at https://link.springer.com/bookseries/8914

Richard Frederick Heller

The Distributed University for Sustainable Higher Education

Springer

Richard Frederick Heller
Milsons Point, NSW, Australia

Richard F Heller

ISSN 2211-1921 ISSN 2211-193X (electronic)
SpringerBriefs in Education
ISBN 978-981-16-6505-9 ISBN 978-981-16-6506-6 (eBook)
https://doi.org/10.1007/978-981-16-6506-6

© The Author(s) 2022. This book is an open access publication.
Open Access This book is licensed under the terms of the Creative Commons Attribution 4.0 International License (http://creativecommons.org/licenses/by/4.0/), which permits use, sharing, adaptation, distribution and reproduction in any medium or format, as long as you give appropriate credit to the original author(s) and the source, provide a link to the Creative Commons license and indicate if changes were made.
The images or other third party material in this book are included in the book's Creative Commons license, unless indicated otherwise in a credit line to the material. If material is not included in the book's Creative Commons license and your intended use is not permitted by statutory regulation or exceeds the permitted use, you will need to obtain permission directly from the copyright holder.
The use of general descriptive names, registered names, trademarks, service marks, etc. in this publication does not imply, even in the absence of a specific statement, that such names are exempt from the relevant protective laws and regulations and therefore free for general use.
The publisher, the authors and the editors are safe to assume that the advice and information in this book are believed to be true and accurate at the date of publication. Neither the publisher nor the authors or the editors give a warranty, expressed or implied, with respect to the material contained herein or for any errors or omissions that may have been made. The publisher remains neutral with regard to jurisdictional claims in published maps and institutional affiliations.

This Springer imprint is published by the registered company Springer Nature Singapore Pte Ltd.
The registered company address is: 152 Beach Road, #21-01/04 Gateway East, Singapore 189721, Singapore

Preface

My life as an educator in the university sector started in 1969 in Chicago when, as a first year resident, I was appointed as an instructor in Medicine. This was an automatic appointment to recognise the role of junior doctors as teachers of medical students, so no credit to me. Since then, I have had more than 50 years working in the higher education sector, including two university chairs at the University of Manchester in the UK and the University of Newcastle in Australia. I had a leadership role in the International Clinical Epidemiology Network—a Rockefeller Foundation funded capacity building programme for 26 medical schools across the developing world. I was the founder and coordinator of a fully online programme to provide master's level Public Health skills for health professionals which has reached more than 100 countries. I have spanned various types of educational offerings, large lectures, small groups, problem based, and online learning. I have also held relatively senior management roles, as head of department, centre director, assistant dean for finance, and deputy dean, but all as additional responsibilities to a primary academic role as teacher and researcher (with around 400 publications in the peer reviewed literature). My field has been health, more specifically epidemiology and Public Health, although I have worked at the clinical coalface as a consultant hospital physician in general medicine. I was in at the start of what has come to be called evidence-based practice—the movement to ensure that evidence underlies practice in the health arena.

I started my personal experience of university education as a medical student in a small medical school, part of the University of London. With 45 students in each year, this was a personalised small group system with a few lectures and few formal assessments other than final examinations. We followed our teachers around their work and picked up what we could.

As a junior doctor, in the USA and the UK, this approach morphed into more of a doing type of apprenticeship system. Learning on the job and quickly moving to teach others—'see one; do one; teach one'.

I was never part of a training programme and just applied for positions that would give me experience and help my progression up the career ladder. Self-study was my method to gain further professional qualifications.

With no formal educational expertise, I was then appointed as a lecturer in another London University medical school and again learned on the job. Attendance at some short courses was followed by self-study to gain a doctorate, personally mentored by a wonderful teacher. Appointment as a senior lecturer at another medical school in London followed and I did some lecturing and small group tutoring while continuing to develop a research portfolio and applying for research grants to support this.

It was a mid-career move to Australia in 1984 that opened my eyes to the importance of educational theory, organisational structure, and global education needs. The appointment was funded by a grant from the Rockefeller Foundation as part of the International Clinical Epidemiology Network, where mid-career clinicians from the developing world were to be given skills in the population health sciences—my first real exposure to the needs for education to boost the global workforce. I found myself at the University of Newcastle in New South Wales, where an exciting educational experiment in active learning—problem based learning—was taking place. During my time in Newcastle, I saw how managers progressively took over university governance and built the importance of the business model, while downgrading academic leadership.

It was in what I thought to be a final career move to the University of Manchester back in the UK that I fully became aware of the dominance of the competitive and managerial business model in the university and the reduced importance of education. The lack of any fundamental attention to environmental sustainability was increasingly apparent. During my time at Manchester, I was able to establish a fully online master's course in Public Health and began to realise the real potential of online learning.

On my retirement from Manchester, the university doubled the fees for overseas students—this not only reinforced my understanding of the reach of the business model but demonstrated the failure of universities to respond to global educational needs. It stimulated me to establish Peoples-uni (http://peoples-uni.org)—aiming to help build Public Health capacity in developing countries through volunteer led online education for health professionals at low cost.

While my career working in university education may be rather more varied than that of some other academics, spanning three continents and 50 years, many others will have drawn similar conclusions from their own experiences. It is my participation in the International Clinical Education Network and Peoples-uni that has given me a global perspective and has led to some potential answers to the problems. I do not suggest that my observations of the individual problems are original, but by bringing them together, I hope to demonstrate the breadth as well as the depth of the issues facing the university sector today. I also believe that I have some solutions that could help improve the situation for the future health of the university sector whose success is so important for us all. These solutions can be applied under any political regime, left or right. I do not propose to stray into the politics of the support for university education in general.

In writing this book, I have tried to take an evidence based approach, and you will see that I do quote the literature extensively in the narrative. However, it is evidence from my experience that forms the basis of what I have written and I have used anecdotes from this to illustrate some of the issues. You will see some general as well as detailed ideas, and while my experience is drawn largely from the health arena, I hope that readers will see the applicability across the university sector.

Milsons Point, Australia   Richard Frederick Heller

Acknowledgements

I would like to thank my wife, Ann, for her unfailing support throughout both the writing of this book and the career that has led to it.

Thanks also to Ann, my daughter Jane Heller, and my friend and colleague Rajan Madhok who each read and commented so helpfully on draft versions of the book and whose discussions have contributed to and enriched my thinking.

Contents

1	**Some Context: From First to Fourth Generation Universities**	1
	References	4
2	**The Problem with Universities Today**	5
	2.1 Managerialism Creates Burdens for Academics with No Evidence of Benefit	6
	2.2 Business Imperatives Override Educational Imperatives	10
	2.3 Needless Competition Between Universities Leads to Duplication	13
	2.4 Research Imperatives, Including for Academic Advancement, Override Educational Reward Systems	15
	2.5 Local Educational Needs are Ignored for Overseas Student Income	19
	2.6 Global Inequalities in Educational Need are Ignored	21
	2.7 Universities have Not Kept Up with the Way Young People Gain Information	26
	2.8 Environmental Sustainability is Ignored	29
	References	34
3	**Solutions**	39
	3.1 Develop Trust in Academic Staff to Replace Managerialism	39
	3.2 Focus on Collaboration—And a New Taxonomy	42
	3.3 A Proposal for an 'International Baccalaureate' for Higher Education	48
	3.4 Utilise Volunteers as Untapped Educators	50
	3.5 Move to Online Learning	53
	3.6 Place Education in a Framework of Environmental Sustainability—The Distributed University	54
	3.7 Use Open Educational Resources	58
	3.8 Take Advantage of Modern Technology and the Fourth Industrial Revolution	61

	3.9	Develop a True Global Perspective to Reduce Global Inequalities in Access to, and Benefits of, Higher Education	63
	3.10	Reduce Reliance on Overseas Student Fees and Develop the 'Global Online Learning' Programme	63
	3.11	Plan E for Education—Increasing Online Public Access to Higher Education	65
	References		69
4	**But How Can We Afford It?**		73
	4.1	Separating Teaching and Research Funds and Functions	73
	4.2	Making Trust the Major Mechanism for Ensuring Quality	74
	4.3	Changing the Educational Process	75
	Reference		76
5	**A Case Study—Peoples-uni, and Conclusions**		77
	5.1	Peoples-uni	77
	5.2	Conclusions	79
	References		80

Chapter 1
Some Context: From First to Fourth Generation Universities

Abstract The evolution and governance of the modern university, the balance between the needs of the consumer (students and employers) and the community (knowledge stock and needs of society).

Keywords Societal needs · University governance · Third generation university

It might be helpful to start by thinking about the role of a university, how it fits into the educational spectrum, how universities evolved and how they work today. In essence, universities take over when school education finishes, and offer people the opportunity to gain a higher academic degree and to perform research.

There is considerable debate about when universities started to exist. What we now know as a university can be traced back to the eleventh twelfth and thirteenth centuries where establishments in Bologna, Paris and Oxford appear to have been the earliest examples (https://www.historyofinformation.com/detail.php?id=4153). Although they were able to award a degree, they were very different organisations from what we now know as a university—they did not own buildings for example. Even earlier, there are examples of institutions where scholars could come together to study—the University of Nalanda started in fifth century India and contained buildings and a library (https://nalandauniversity.wordpress.com/about/) and the University of al-Qarawiyyin in Fez, Morocco was founded in the ninth century and has been going ever since (https://en.m.wikipedia.org/wiki/University_of_al-Qarawiyyin). Many of these had religious underpinnings.

The early universities seemed to focus on education, and have been termed first generation universities. Along with the enlightenment the next, second, generation iteration added research to education. Those were the simple days.

The third generation universities (Wissema 2009), discovered that there were ways of adding value to teaching and research—they could have a role in building national capacities, be involved in policy generation, and they could partner with actors outside the university sector. Enter the commercialisation of education and research, the involvement of entrepreneurs, and the creation of the professional university administrator to cope with increasing student numbers. As you will see in the next chapter, it is the managerial consequences of these developments that created many of the problems which we continue to experience.

© The Author(s) 2022
R. F. Heller, *The Distributed University for Sustainable Higher Education*,
SpringerBriefs in Education, https://doi.org/10.1007/978-981-16-6506-6_1

It might be useful at the start of this book to summarise the place of universities in the education system, and how universities function, although I suspect that most readers will be familiar with this. Terminology varies, and we should understand that there are many types of post-school education, usually defined as 'higher education'. The university sector is only a part of this. Education for trades maybe offered through apprenticeships to a skilled tradesman, or courses run by different bodies, and there are various ways of gaining certification of such training. This is often called vocational education and training. In Australia, for example, there is a system of Technical and Further Education (TAFE) which provides qualification awards. There is usually a national qualifications framework which defines various levels of post-school education, and national bodies that accredit organisations to provide education at these levels.

Professional bodies offer education and training towards professional accreditation, so that lawyers, accountants, architects, veterinarians, medical specialists etc. can be accredited and work in their various professions at an appropriate and accredited level. Universities may collaborate with and provide some of this professional education.

Thinking back to my own education after leaving school, it has been a mixture of apprenticeship, university education and professional accreditation.

Universities provide undergraduate education, and then graduates have the opportunity to enrol in postgraduate education. Awards at the undergraduate level are called bachelor's degrees, and postgraduate awards may be certificate, diploma, master's or doctoral degrees. The ability to award a degree is key to the importance of the university sector. Accreditation is granted to individual universities by national regulatory authorities, according to agreed criteria, which also apply to a review and renewal process.

The possession of a university degree is key to advancement to the next stage on the academic ladder for those who want a higher degree, and to professional advancement for many people. Beyond the role of a university degree in the career development of individuals, we should also ask about the overall purpose of universities for society. Is it to increase the stock of knowledge and disseminate it to improve society, or to give people the skills for the jobs they will have in the future? Put simply—are the drivers of the university sector consumer or community? Once the consumer, student or employer, is the driver, we run into the need to market and to compete. Forstenzer (2017) puts it nicely *"Allowing universities to be defined primarily by their capacity to meet market criteria (such as balancing the books and delivering customer satisfaction) is a radical departure from the idea that universities exist to serve the public."*

In the diagram, I have shown the balance between consumer and community in driving university priorities. Failure to achieve an appropriate balance between these has led to many of the problems I am going to describe in later chapters (Fig. 1.1).

The consumer driven approach leads to competition between providers, and requires a business-type model, which then defines the way that universities are managed and governed. In most countries, the governance of universities is overseen by a university council or board. Council members may come from local or national

1 Some Context: From First to Fourth Generation Universities

Competing drivers of the university sector

Fig. 1.1 Competing drivers of the university sector

organisations, including industry and academia, and will be chosen according to the skill set they can provide. The council's main job is to set overall strategy and appoint the chief executive officer (vice-chancellor or president) who will then be key to appointing the other senior executives such as deputy and pro vice-chancellors. If the Council, and the vice-chancellor appointed by the Council, have a business focus, that will set the scene for the way the university is run.

The governance structure within each university varies somewhat between different universities and also globally, and covers academic and business governance. Usual structures have the university divided into faculties which have a common set of interests—such as health, or humanities, or science—which are themselves split into more focused schools and then departments. Each has their own administrative structure including academics, such as deans and administrative support staff. Educational governance comes through university-wide committees, and committees in each of the faculties, schools and departments. There are also university-wide administrative structures to support finances, human resources, educational design and research infrastructure. This all usually involves a top down centralised oversight 'command and control' structure, with limited autonomy for faculties and schools and even less for departments and individual academics. Where historically the university was run by academics, it is the administrators who now have the leading management role.

Most universities offer a similar suite of courses, and span teaching and research, although there are a few specialised universities. Academic members of staff are expected to split their time between teaching, research and 'service', although the proportional split varies and there are a few teaching only and research only appointments. As we will see later, criteria for appointments and promotions depend on performance in these various roles.

Beyond the notions of individual university governance, and national accrediting bodies who attempt to ensure quality, there are broader issues to consider. All countries provide funding for the university sector, and direct their funding in a way that attempts to meet national needs. The extent of this government support (and control) varies, as does the mix between public and private universities and the reliance on student fees. Going back to the notion of consumer or community, the greater the proportionate government input into funding, the greater can be the attempt to meet government perceptions of national and community needs—according to its political priorities. But how do other broader societal values such as fairness and equity, in particular global inequalities in access to education, and environmental sustainability find their way into university governance?

This scene setting has identified many of these themes that are picked up later in the book, which I hope will help us prepare for the next, fourth, generation of universities.

References

Forstenzer J. We are losing sight of higher education's true purpose. The Conversation; 2017. https://theconversation.com/we-are-losing-sight-of-higher-educations-true-purpose-73637.
Nalanda University. https://nalandauniversity.wordpress.com/about/.
Norman J. The Universitas Guild: Early Origin of What We Characterize as a University. History of Information.com. https://www.historyofinformation.com/detail.php?id=4153.
University of al-Qarawiyyin. https://en.m.wikipedia.org/wiki/University_of_al-Qarawiyyin.
Wissema JG. Towards the Third Generation University: managing the University in transition. Edward Elgar Pub; 2009.

Open Access This chapter is licensed under the terms of the Creative Commons Attribution 4.0 International License (http://creativecommons.org/licenses/by/4.0/), which permits use, sharing, adaptation, distribution and reproduction in any medium or format, as long as you give appropriate credit to the original author(s) and the source, provide a link to the Creative Commons license and indicate if changes were made.

The images or other third party material in this chapter are included in the chapter's Creative Commons license, unless indicated otherwise in a credit line to the material. If material is not included in the chapter's Creative Commons license and your intended use is not permitted by statutory regulation or exceeds the permitted use, you will need to obtain permission directly from the copyright holder.

Chapter 2
The Problem with Universities Today

Abstract Managerialism creates burdens for academics with no evidence for its benefit. Business imperatives override educational. There is needless competition between universities. Research imperatives override education. Global inequalities in educational need are ignored, universities have not kept up with the way young people gain information and initiatives to reduce the environmental impact of higher education are 'tinkering' rather than the required total re-thinking of higher education.

Keywords Academic · Universities · Managerialism · Global inequalities · Collaboration · Environmental sustainability

The first section identifies some of the key problems associated with the universities of today, from the perspective of the academic. After all it is the academic staff, the teachers and researchers, who are the people without whom the university cannot function. Universities contain so many excellent and committed academics, creating the next generation of educated members of society and performing wonderful research to underpin our future, that I do not want this to sound too negative and I do want to pay my respects to the excellence that does exist in universities at all levels. However identification and dissection of the problem is the first step in finding solutions.

I have started with managerialism, as this is what drives the unhappiness of so many academics. The chapter continues with the issues of industrialisation and commercialisation of universities—of course these are bound up with managerialism as the sector regards itself as an industry and industries have managers. Then follows a digression to discuss the way in which universities, initially created to teach, have evolved a hierarchy which places research above teaching, and in the process downgrades its core teaching business. Tied up with commercialisation is the problem created by the lure of fees from international students, cruelly exposed by the Covid-19 pandemic which at the time of writing has reduced global travel to the extent that it has put many university academics out of work. Before Covid-19, the focus on international students had, perversely, ignored the real global inequalities in access to education and had skewed educational priorities within the countries to which international students come. This leads on to a discussion of how universities have not kept up with changes in the way that young people learn, and finally how they have ignored the massive and growing need for environmental sustainability. This chapter is really to set the scene for the following chapter on solutions—which I propose for each of the problems identified.

2.1 Managerialism Creates Burdens for Academics with No Evidence of Benefit

My exposure to the issue of the increasing role of the manager in university structures started at the University of Newcastle in Australia. As Professor of Community Medicine, I held a large capacity building grant from the Rockefeller Foundation for many years. Initially, I was allowed to administer the funds, use them to work out the spread of academic and support staff required to meet our obligations under the grant, and advertise, interview and appoint the relevant people. This was done in accordance with University processes, but in the context of the needs of the grant and based on the internal processes within our group. Since this was a capacity building programme, the development and delivery of courses was fundamental to the work, and we were able to decide on the need for, and methods to, adapt the courses. We developed a completely new adaptation to a distance learning format, and we could add and subtract courses as the breadth of the programme grew. The programme was aimed at developing countries, and travel was an essential component. We were also able to book our own travel, using a self-selected travel agent (in the days when these existed) with whom we developed a close working relationship and who knew and was able to respond to our needs.

Over time, the independence that we had experienced was eroded, the grant was subsumed into the general funds of the University and appointments were made by the University. The carrot held out was that if we lost the grant, the funds for the salaries would be underwritten, at least for the length of the contract and we would have security. However, we lost the ability to respond to the direct needs of the grant, and had the extra burden of the paperwork and discussions and meetings required by the University in seeking approvals at each step. We also lost the ability to tailor our travel requirements to our needs—for no obvious benefit. These examples of managers replacing individual academic independence would seem trivial in comparison with examples of managerial oversight at which any university academic could point today. However they might serve as an illustration of a turning point in academia.

The Oxford English Dictionary defines managerialism as *"belief in or reliance on the use of professional managers in administering or planning an activity"*. The word 'belief' in this definition is indicative of the fact that universities have adopted managerialism in the absence of evidence. Deem (1998) defines 'new managerialism' as *"the adoption by public sector organisations of organisational forms, technologies, management practices and values more commonly found in the private business sector."* She goes on to equate new managerialism with the 'hard' form of managerialism which involves rewards and punishments for those who can't be trusted, and

2.1 Managerialism Creates Burdens for Academics …

suggests that this is a masculine approach as opposed to the more feminist collegiality or 'soft' management approach. The issue of trust is key here—and I will be making the case later on that trust in academics is the alternative to managerialism which we need to explore. Deem and Brehony (2005) call 'new managerialism' an ideology "*to serve the interests of manager academics and help cement relations of power and dominance, even in contexts like universities which were not traditionally associated with the dominance of management*".

Some history of how managerialism developed is also helpful to understand the issue. Davies (2003) identifies that "*New managerialism, which is also referred to as neo-liberalism in the UK and total quality management in the USA, is a system of government of individuals invented during the Thatcher and Reagan years. It may well involve the most significant shift in the discursive construction of professional practice and professional responsibility that any of us will ever experience. It is characterised by the removal of the locus of power from the knowledge of practising professionals to auditors, policy-makers and statisticians, none of whom need know anything about the profession in question (Rose 1999). Neo-liberalism is characterised by Thatcher's 'death of society' and the rise of 'individuals' who are in need of management, surveillance and control.*" One of the key aspects of managerialism is the notion that there are generic skills that a manager has that can be applied in any organisation.

Managerialism, which was designed to improve performance in public services, has been adopted uncritically by universities. I can find no evidence of the benefit of this approach, nor even of any attempts to evaluate its benefit. As Shepherd suggests (2018), even its theoretical construct is poorly defined. Shepherd also reports a survey of a number of senior university managers which shows that they "*appear to have fully accepted the idea that university management is both necessary and beneficial*"—at least managers think that management is important! Aspromourgos (2012) suggests that there is no economic case for the managerial approach "*a quality university product, of research plus teaching plus service, cannot be reduced to key performance indicators, and therefore its provision cannot be ensured merely by recourse to more or less explicit individual contracts….Not only are managerialism and quasi-competition not substitutes for traditional quality assurance grounded in professional ethics, they serve to undermine it*".

McKenna (2018) refers to the changes associated with managerialism as 'bureaucratic bloat' and says: "*The issue is that introducing significant, expensive administrative structures too often comes at the cost of the pursuit and development of knowledge…The blame for this bloat of bureaucracy doesn't only rest with executive administrators. Academics have ceded the academic project to the empty rhetoric of efficiency.*" As Graeber in Bullshit Jobs laments (2019), this has led to an explosion of jobs for managers. Over time this growth has outstripped the growth of academic jobs in universities.

Having created new jobs in management, the people holding the jobs have to find work to do. However, this involves not only the managers themselves, but the academics—more forms to fill and meetings to attend. As infrastructure jobs are reduced over time it is the academics who have to do all this work, adding to or replacing their academic workload. Orr and Orr (2016) give some delightful examples of the expansion of tasks given to the academics under what they define as *'managerialism, metrics and bureaucratisation (MMB)'*. The figures, reproduced from their paper (with permission) compare the tasks under MMB (on the left) compared without MMB (on the right) in authorising travel and creating an exam (Figs. 2.1 and 2.2).

Having put managers at the top of the university hierarchy, the academics find themselves undervalued by all levels of university administration. If a low level member of the research administration demands some paperwork from the academic, this becomes a requirement to be met, not questioned, despite any doubts from the academic. Timetabling becomes a task for the academic, not the manager, despite this taking time and energy away from teaching and research.

As well as adding to the academics' workload and taking them away from teaching and research. The academics suffer from lack of control over their own activities. Control is exerted by others who are neither expert in their field nor have experience

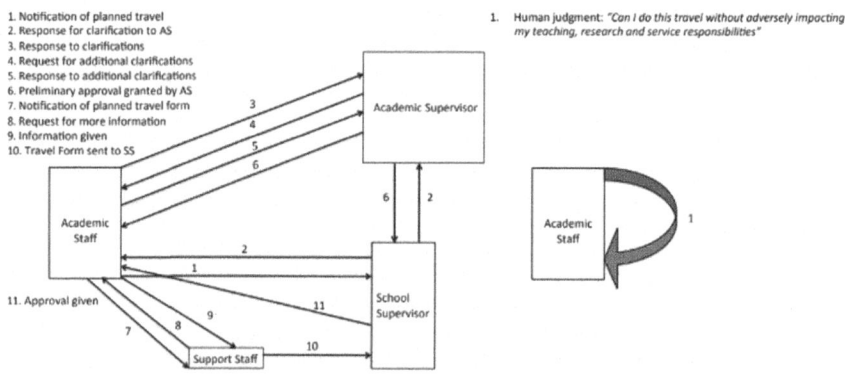

Fig. 2.1 Numbers of emails sent in the process travel authorisation outside the semester

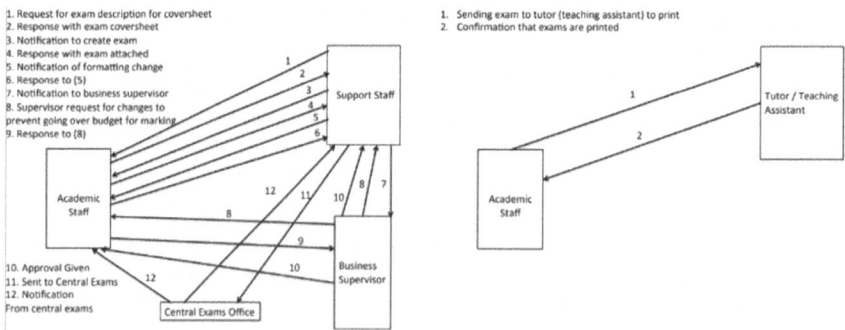

Fig. 2.2 Numbers of emails sent in the process of the creation of an exam

in the provision of education or conduct of research. Locus of control is a psychological concept—the lack of which has been identified to create stress and anxiety. As summarised by Whitehead and colleagues (2016) *"Observational evidence showed that employees who experienced the twin pressures of high job demands but low control in their work were at higher risk of psychosocial stress, which has been linked to physical conditions such as coronary heart disease (CHD)"*. These twin pressures are just what so many of today's academics face—largely as a result of managerialism.

A number of authors tell us that managerialism a form of bullying. David West has said in a provocative piece in the Sydney Morning Herald (2015) *"The increasing incidence of bullying over the last few decades coincides with the relentless rise of managerialism....Why does the current model of managerialism almost inevitably give rise to cases of bullying? University reforms of the last decades have been driven by neoliberal assumptions or what has misleadingly been called economic rationalism: the primacy of economic principles of productivity and efficiency; the central role of management and incentives."*

Skinner and colleagues in a study of bullying and harassment in Australian universities (Skinner et al. 2015) says: *"All these findings point to organisational culture, whether driven from within or from without, as important in understanding harassment and bullying in the workplace....These health impacts would then be expected to result in increased absenteeism, lower job satisfaction and lower morale. These have organisation-related effects, with workplace bullying damaging productivity and reputation. The diverse range of costs organisations incur can include lost productivity, the cost of replacement workers when victims are absent, recruitment costs resulting from higher staff turnover, the costs of processing formal complaints and lost business due to reputation loss"*.

Salin (2003) proposed a model to explain workplace bullying with three components: *"enabling structures or necessary antecedents (e.g. perceived power imbalances, low perceived costs, and dissatisfaction and frustration), motivating structures or incentives (e.g. internal competition, reward systems and expected benefits), and precipitating processes or triggering circumstances (e.g. downsizing and restructuring, organizational changes, changes in the composition of the work group)."* Each of these might be relevant to the university setting.

Keashly and Neuman (2015) blame the organisation's workplace competitive culture with leadership that does not tolerate nonconformity for breeding bullying and hostile behaviour at work, and conclude that *"These are conditions that appear contrary to the academy's espoused notions of collegiality and civility, grounded in the "sacred" values of academic freedom and autonomy."*

I am sure that university managers do not see themselves as bullies, and may themselves feel hostage to the managerial approach. Some of the blame comes from outside the individual universities themselves. Various countries have imposed research assessment exercises where universities are graded, and ranked, according to their research output—which then has an influence on funding to the university. As well as causing the university to take a more authoritarian management style, this promotes competition between and within universities.

Burnes et al. (2014) succinctly describe the change in power and control within modern universities with the observation that *"successive governments cutting universities' funding and compelling them to act more like business enterprises than educational institutions. In turn, vice-chancellors have become more similar to powerful chief executives, collegial forms of control have been significantly reduced and academic staff increasingly work in an environment in which they are told what to teach, how to teach, what research to conduct and where to publish."*

Some commentators are very hard on the senior university management. Ericson et al. (2020) performed a large survey of UK academics and found a mean satisfaction score of only 10%. Their further analysis of drivers for dissatisfaction in this population *"revealed seven major themes: the dominance and brutality of metrics; excessive workload; governance and accountability; perpetual change; vanity projects; the silenced academic; work and mental health"* The authors conclude that *"Managerial oversight of academic work has reached a critical tipping point. Extensive auditing of research output by means of performance management assessment regimes motivated by a New Public Management mentality has damaged individual scholarship and threatened academic freedom"* and they quote Craig et al. (2014) who *"characterise university senior management regimes as supporting courts of conformers and colluders who are selfish, ambitious and openly supportive of toxic tyrants where universities, bedevilled by audit culture, are characterised as psychotic."* Support for this harsh assessment of university culture is also offered by Halffman and Radder (2015), who observe that *"the university has been occupied by the many-headed Wolf of management (which has) colonised academia with a mercenary army of professional administrators…Management has proclaimed academics the enemy within: academics cannot be trusted, and so have to be tested and monitored, under the permanent threat of reorganisation, termination and dismissal."*

The key problem seems to be that universities have adopted a management style used in much of the public and private sectors without evidence of its effectiveness or recognition of the special circumstances of academia. Compounding this, most university managers do not actually have management training.

This is not just an internal matter for how universities work and treat their staff. It is the senior managers, perhaps driven on by or at least in acquiescence from the university governing bodies or councils, who have developed the competitive business models that I also identify as part of the problem in the next few sections.

2.2 Business Imperatives Override Educational Imperatives

At the University of Newcastle in New South Wales, Australia, where I spent 17 very happy and productive years, a new Vice Chancellor (head person in the administrative chain of the UK style university) was appointed. His deputy held an informal meeting to introduce him to some of the senior academic staff. When my turn came to be introduced—"This is Dick Heller—he breaks all the rules of the

University, but we don't mind because he brings in a lot of money". I was not sure of which part of the description I should be most proud.

Underpinning the way that third generation universities developed, universities have become businesses. The driver is the perception that this is in order to survive financially, although in reality it reflects a perception that universities have to become 'modern' and reflect other trends in society. The managerialism and competition we have been discussing need to be seen in this context—each of which are requirements of a business ethos.

Kellerman puts the issue nicely (Kellermann 2011) *"Whereas the business world counts its output by surpluses and deficits in statistics of money, the university system sees its results in scientific findings, publications and reputation."* He compares the *"university as a business"* with the *"university of the mind"*, and reflects on the tendency of contemporary society to turn as many things as possible into commodities and concludes: *"There is no doubt: In a money society the university also needs money like every citizen. But it definitely makes a difference if the primary purpose of an organisation is to make money profit as in the case of commercial business or if it is to make profit in knowledge as the authentic university."*

This brings us back to the wider purpose of the university, as Scott identifies (2015): *"...we seem to be increasingly losing our sense of public responsibility and wider social purpose"*.

One consequence is that financially unrewarding parts of university activities are at risk of being sacrificed in favour of those that create income.

The Los Angeles Times (Hiltzik 2016) regrets that *"Students already are losing out. They're not only saddled with an increasing share of the direct costs of their education, but are offered a narrower curriculum as universities cut back on supposedly unprofitable humanities and social science courses in favor of science, engineering and technology programs expected to attract profitable grants and offer the prospects of great riches from patentable inventions....What's really at stake in the corporatization of academia is the traditional role the university as a repository of culture and training ground for open inquiry."* The article quotes Michael Meranze (https://utotherescue.blogspot.com) *"The obvious risk is that academic research gets done to advance the interests of outside corporations, rather than guided by the logic of the university's mission."*

There is a great deal of sympathy for the university which has to survive—as Scott (2015) admits *"It would be naive to pretend it will be easy to reclaim that sense of public responsibility. The pressures on universities, and especially their leaders, to embrace corporate values and adopt quasi-business strategies are enormous."*

But where is the pressure to turn things around? Academics have lost power within the institution, and are fearful about stepping out of line especially as tenured posts with their job security are less common, and the managerialism previously discussed creates penalties and rewards. A senior academic at Murdoch University in Western Australia complained publicly that the University was lowering its academic standards for fee paying overseas students. He was censured, and sued, by the University for bringing it into disrepute, and other Australian universities were concerned that this could hurt their ability to attract overseas students—and the money they bring in (Zaglas 2019). However, at least in Australia, academics are trying to fight back. An open letter is described in this article in the Conversation 'Universities are not corporations': 600 Australian academics call for change to uni governance structures (Pelizzon et al. 2020), which identifies the dangers of the corporatisation of the university and suggests a change to a more democratic and horizontal management structure.

As governments try to save costs, in many countries they have demanded that a larger portion of university costs should be bourne by the students. In both the UK and Australia for example governments changed from free provision of university education to demanding student fees—with increases over time to be offset by student loans that could be repaid once the graduates earn enough. In the United States student fees are much higher in private universities, but students at public universities still have to pay fees. In Scandinavia, universities are funded by the government rather than asking for contributions from students. Of course these decisions by governments reflect larger political agendas, but requiring that students pay fees helps to create a scenario where universities adopt a business stance and compete for consumers, rather than cooperate with each other.

This brings me to discuss the overseas student 'market' for the fees they attract. We will discuss this in the context of global inequalities in educational opportunity in a later chapter, but in many countries now overseas student fees account for a large proportion of university finances. In Australia, overseas students became the third largest 'export' earners—behind iron ore and coal mining. Again this creates the imperative to compete and to adopt a business mentality.

Here is a media release from Universities Australia—'The voice of Australian Universities' (International students inject $32 billion a year into Australia's economy—boosting Aussie jobs and wages 2018) headed: International students injected $31.9 billion into Australia's economy last financial year, directly boosting Australian jobs and wages—including in regional Australia.

> The latest Australian Bureau of Statistics figures – released today – confirm international education income grew by $3.8 billion in the financial year to June 2018 to reach $31.9 billion… Universities Australia Deputy Chief Executive Anne-Marie Lansdown said a record 548,000 international students were now studying in Australia, with the majority enrolled at universities. "Our world-class universities attract students from all over the globe, bringing vast benefits to Australians and the nation," Ms Lansdown said. "And the buck doesn't stop with us – that $32 billion flows on into the entire Australian economy, generating jobs, supporting wages, and lifting the living standards of Australians." "International education is a modern Australian success story – built from the ground up over six decades to become the nation's third-largest export and the envy of the world."

The business approach determines that education now becomes a commodity to be bought and sold. As Kellerman says: *"Commodities require markets for selling and buying. In order to be able to sell and to buy something, it must be produced. The purpose of production is no longer primarily to meet the diversity of human needs but to make money…the university is no longer an institution for young people to study in order to broaden and deepen their knowledge or for qualified people to undertake research or for teachers to educate all kinds of interested people. Instead studying, researching and teaching at the university are becoming instruments for making money. This reduction of purposes and functions of the university has consequences for the people involved and for the results as well. Initially intrinsically motivated persons are now focused on obtaining a qualification or even on getting only a certification, a label, in order to earn money at a later stage."*

There is little debate about the impact on the higher education sector and broader society of these issues, other than at election time where the debate is curtailed and usually superficial. Should other countries follow the Scandinavian model of public funding for the majority of university costs? What would be the impact on equality of access to higher education from such a model? Are there other possible funding models? Turning universities into businesses has a whole range of consequences for society—beyond the consequences for the universities themselves. Where is this debate being held—other than in various blogs by concerned academics?

The consquence of the business model is the drive to compete, as discussed in this next section.

2.3 Needless Competition Between Universities Leads to Duplication

After Australia, when I arrived at the University of Manchester in the UK, I saw first hand the competitive ethos that had developed between even neighbouring universities. Stimulated by my earlier experience of online education in Newcastle, and following a promise at my interview for the position, I started to develop a new fully online master's course in Public Health. Within a few miles of Manchester, a number of other universities were offering courses in Public Health, and one was also planning to develop an online version. I suggested that the two of us could combine to develop a world class online course building on the strengths and infrastructure of both institutions. But they preferred to compete rather than combine, so we each developed our courses independently, duplicating the work and competing for students. In fact, they outsourced their course development and maintenance to a private commercial organisation, costing them and their students a lot of money, rather than collaborate with us.

Competition is supposed to increase quality, as in theory the better courses will attract more students. There are two things wrong with this in relation to higher education, in addition to the lack of evidence for the idea in the first place. First, and most important, is that competition *between* universities does not improve the population's access to education or research output in relation to the population's needs, it just shifts the load between the different universities. Second, the main metrics to measure and compare universities relate to research output—there being little evidence that research output and teaching excellence are related. The competition game requires measurement to make comparisons—this not only means finding appropriate metrics but also requires an infrastructure to make the measures.

Competition is rife between universities, and I can see that where there is no cap on student numbers, and universities get funding per student, there may be a drive to compete to attract students. For example in recent years both the UK and Australian governments removed the cap on undergraduate student numbers (in Australia the next government re-introduced a cap).

There is also competition to attract staff, and in a further example from my Manchester experience, the Vice Chancellor at the time was fixated on attracting Nobel Prize winners to the staff. The University boasts 25 Nobel Laureates amongst its current and former staff and students, and while some of these were 'home grown' others were bought in, some for only a portion of their time after the prize had been awarded. What does that do for the global research effort? Nothing, as these researchers and their teams would have done the same work elsewhere. Naidoo puts it well (Naidoo 2016) *"The competition fetish also threatens academics' capacity to work towards global well-being. Much research and policy focuses on how universities contribute to the economic and social development of their own countries. But many of the major issues facing humankind – the destruction of the environment, rising inequality and violence across borders – can only be solved by countries and universities working together. In this sense, the question of how higher education contributes to global well-being becomes very important."*

The high salaries paid to induce high flyers reduces the amount available to the rest of the university, creating resentment along the way. *"The downside is not just an unequal distribution of social opportunities..., but the isolation of many of the fruits of intellectual life in a handful of hard-to-enter institutions. The steeper the distance between elite universities and others, the more that society values elite universities and the less it sees of their benefits. This is the logic of a winner-take-all market..."* Marginson (2006).

Naidoo also states that the competition fetish and may be applied uncritically. She identifies a number of unintended consequences: *"Competition threatens academic work by setting up research excellence frameworks that result in unintended consequences. There is evidence for this: Germany's "Excellence Initiative" has resulted in more stratification, a downgrading of teaching and an additional administrative burden. Such frameworks also militate against "blue skies" research – the sort that is driven by curiosity rather than a production agenda. These frameworks encourage dubious research tactics for maximising citations. They over-emphasise conformity to politically expedient external expectations."* We will return to the research excellence frameworks later.

Musselin tells us (2018): *"Not only have competition and competitive schemes dramatically developed in the last decades, from competition for students to competition for budgets and competition for professors, but the nature of competition has also evolved, leading to new forms of competition, especially on the segment where this evolution has been the strongest, i.e. research universities. It is argued that competition in higher education is no longer only occurring between individuals and countries, but has become institutional, leading to a multi-level form of competition and transforming universities into competitors. This competition is framed as*

2.3 Needless Competition Between Universities Leads to Duplication

a competition for quality which has become more organized and equipped, and that increasingly relies on impersonal judgment devices."

Musselin again: *"Meanwhile, the notion of knowledge economy, which became a buzzword in the 1990s, recast research outcomes as potential goods with economic value and as major drivers of economic development… This is often described as the commodification or economization of higher education, since an economic value is attributed to all and everything, including research and teaching…"* Creating education as a commodity, commodification, has other major consequences—to which we will also return later.

The competition game is one example of how the higher education sector has uncritically adopted emerging societal trends without considering if they are relevant and appropriate to the sector. Australia, with its smallish population, at the last count had 28 Master of Public Health courses in separate higher education institutions. How much duplication of effort has been wasted to develop and maintain all these courses, instead of sharing? How many courses are needed? What areas relevant to public health are missed due to everyone teaching the same thing and competing with each other for the same student body? How many public health graduates are needed? Should we not be taking a population view of needs (a common approach in Public Health) rather than observing needless competition between universities?

Of course it can work both ways, when universities close ranks and collaborate to reduce competition from outside the traditional education sector, such as the private sector. In the UK, the National Health Service attempted to establish its own 'university' to train the health service providers it needed. It faced opposition from the UK higher education sector and was closed down. So the sector can work together to face down external threats, even as it competes internally. There are many other examples of where universities work together to protect the 'brand' at the macro level, to lobby for legislation or funds from governments. It is a shame that this cannot be more effectively transposed across the sphere of teaching and research, and I have some solutions to propose later in the book.

As well as competition between universities as part of the business model, it is also seen within universities. One major example is the competition between education and research, which is the topic of the next section.

2.4 Research Imperatives, Including for Academic Advancement, Override Educational Reward Systems

The University of Manchester was, and is, a prestigious university priding itself on a high reputation and position in global rankings. I discovered that in order to allow the academic staff to focus on research, the Medical School actually contracted out its basic science teaching to another faculty, an early indication of the priority given to research over teaching. Status within the University was very clearly dependent on attracting research grants as evidenced in a number of other ways. Of course this is not restricted to any one university—look at the biographical sketches of staff in many universities and see the boasting of the numbers of millions of dollars earned in research grants. Earlier, while working at the University of Newcastle, I was interviewed for an external research grant, and was asked how I could find the time for research since the Medical School was known for its emphasis on education. Can an academic do both teaching and research? What is the nexus between research and education in the modern university?

As we saw in the section on the history of universities, education was the way that the first generation universities started, and a research function was added later for the second generation. Today, highly research active universities have become the elite of the university world, and within the universities themselves, success in research outcome (defined by grant income and publications) is key to promotion. So how and why did research become the more prestigious end of university activity? My answer has two pretty simple parts—you can get grants for research so it brings in money, and you can measure research outcome (as defined above in terms of grant income and publications—if not in terms of improvements to the community) more easily than educational outcomes. Does society need research or education more? Are there better ways of organising education and research than combining them in institutions and individuals who do both?

It still makes logical sense to me that education should be the 'core business' of the higher education sector. After all, it is not called the 'higher research' sector. So why is the reward system within universities targeted towards the non-core activity? Would a real business create such an inefficient reward system? The story told by those who support the dual role for education and research among the academics themselves and within the universities where they work, is that it is important to incorporate research into teaching and the active researcher will be more up to date than non-researchers. But where is the evidence for that?

Figlio and Schapiro (2017) find in an elite US University that "*...regardless of our measure of teaching quality or our measure of research quality employed, there is no relationship between the teaching quality and research quality of tenured Northwestern faculty...It appears that, at least in the scope of teaching by tenure line Northwestern faculty, the factors that drive teaching excellence and those that determine research excellence appear unrelated.*"

Norton and colleagues (2013) concur, reporting a study from Australian and US sectors: "*Better research does not necessarily lead to better teaching. Original empirical analysis conducted for this report investigated the effect of research on teaching. It found that students in high research departments have very similar experiences to students in low-research departments.*"

Palali and colleagues (2018) report similar findings from the Netherlands: "*We investigate the relationship between research quality and teaching quality, by comparing students that follow the same course, taught by different teachers. We use publication records of teachers as a measure for research quality. Teaching quality is measured by both student evaluations of the teachers and by final student grades. Having any publications at all or total number of publications does not have a significant effect on student grades. We find that being taught by teachers with high quality publications leads to higher grades only for master students. This is not fully reflected in the student evaluations of teachers. Master students do not give higher scores to teachers with high quality of publications, bachelor students give lower scores."*

Norton again: *"Academics are typically appointed for their subject expertise, with much less attention given to their teaching skills. Most academics have no training in teaching or have taken only short courses. Universities outsource large amounts of teaching to casual staff. Many academics prefer research to teaching."*

Elsewhere, Norton (2013) states that Australian universities ... *"... are all more likely to promote academics to senior positions based on research rather than teaching performance. They are all happy for temporary staff to do much of the teaching…This is a common culture across Australia's universities, whether they score highly in research ratings or not."*

Encouraging teaching through reward systems, creating more teaching-only roles within universities and separating institutions into research and teaching organisations have all been suggested. Norton et al. (2013) again: *"Teaching-only universities are occasionally proposed as a solution. But this report's findings suggest that removing research would not on its own solve the teaching problem. Departments that research less have not compensated by building specialisation in teaching. They have similar staffing profiles and practices to departments that research more ..."* He prefers to increase the number of teaching only academic staff members: *"Universities have long required research qualifications, sought research talent, and promoted their most able researchers. Teaching-focused academics can help lead a university culture shift that will make teaching an equal partner with research."*

Each year there are various ranking exercises published, for example the Times Higher Education World University Rankings. While teaching is one of the performance indicators, and accounts for 30% of the ranking score, this indicator actually includes the proportion of research students. 60% of the ranking score comes from research and citations of research publications, so the ranking is very heavily weighted towards research.

Bennett et al. (2017) warns in an article 'Teaching only (TA) roles could mark the end of your academic career' that while teaching academic roles have increased recently in Australian universities, *"these roles can be a negative career move for academics."* University rankings mainly involve some form of a research assessment exercise, with the reward systems for the institution, so *"Higher education needs balanced national and international policy that overcomes the inferior status of teaching in ranking exercises. Without these supports, TA roles present a risk to individual and professional well being and the loss of experienced academics from the sector."*

Of course as Bennett warns, teachers should not neglect to research their own teaching and *"All higher education teachers need to engage in research within and about their discipline."*

Not everyone agrees that universities are the best place for research. In 'If you love research, academia may not be for you' Mathews (2018) tells us that *"Dutch figures show just how little time professors get for their own research. It may be easier to pursue your intellectual interests outside the university system*". He quotes a report from the Netherlands by the Rathenau Instituut (Koens et al. 2018) *"Those lucky enough to have become full professors – supposedly the light at the end of the tunnel for struggling junior scholars – spend just 17 per cent of their time on their own research. Teaching, research supervision and "management and organisational tasks" were all bigger commitments. Associate and assistant professors fare little better carving out research time for themselves...On average, full professors work 45 per cent longer than their contracted hours – assuming a 38-h contract, as the report does, that means a 55-h working week, or an 11-h working day. Those at the assistant and associate professor level put in an extra 29 per cent on top of their contracted hours. Let's run the numbers on these. If the average full professor is working a 55-h week, and spends 17 per cent of their time on research, they get about 9 h 20 min a week to pursue their own research interests."*

So, we reward good researchers at the expense of good teachers, but give them so much other work to do that they do not have time to do their research. The system is broke! If the data presented above are generalisable to other settings, this suggest that the managerialism about which I have been complaining is ineffective in creating appropriate division of activities of the academics. Reducing the large administrative load might free up research time.

On the other hand, there is anecdotal evidence of students hardly seeing tenured senior academics during their time at university as teaching is devolved to higher degree students and contract teaching staff. Less teaching allows more time to be spent on research or administration. I realise that in my suggestion to replace managerialism with trust, the onus will be on the academics to divide their time appropriately. Of course a reduction in managerialism will free up the time that academics currently spend on administration, and allow them to get back to teaching.

The UK adopted the Research Assessment Exercise, and later replaced it with the Research Excellence Framework, to reward the institutions that score highly. Large flows of funding follow high scoring institutions. To try to recognise teaching as well, a Teaching Excellence Framework was established. Yet to be fully evaluated, it has been criticised as using flawed metrics and providing very limited incentives to the institutions that score highly.

While there have been a number of attempts to improve teaching and its rewards, Chalmers (2019) concludes that the examples she has identified from universities in *"... the US, UK, Europe and Australia lead to the same conclusion – good teaching remains largely undervalued, poorly recognised and unrewarded, despite significant investment and initiatives from government and funding bodies over three decades. More concerning is that institutions have failed to link the quality of teaching and the quality of student learning and engagement, despite the strong evidence that has consistently demonstrated the relationship"*.

In a number of countries, such as the UK and Australia, the research carried out in universities is subsidised by earnings from teaching. This is particularly relevant as a major part of this comes from profits made from overseas student fees. At the time of writing the replacement of overseas students by local students as a result of the Covid-19 pandemic will lead to a loss of income and the inability to keep funding research infrastructure. Unless research costs are fully supported by the research funding agencies, and there is clear separation of funding for each type of activity, teaching will continue to be regarded as a second class activity and research will suffer from being dependent on teaching income.

Again we see the importance and the dangers of the business model, amplified in the sections below on overseas student fee income.

2.5 Local Educational Needs are Ignored for Overseas Student Income

I have previously mentioned my personal experience at the University of Newcastle, Australia of holding a large grant from the Rockefeller Foundation that required us to take students from developing countries to assist with building their research capacity (actually it was that grant that brought me to Australia from London). Although we did spend a great deal of time and energy teaching these students, and travelling to interview them and support them on their return, we did also use the grant to employ more academic staff. We were thus able to open the educational programme to local students. So this was an example of a real benefit to local students from the income from overseas students (whether this is an ethical use of funds given to build capacity in developing countries is another issue).

Today, or at least until today given the disruption caused by the Covid-19 pandemic, there are high proportions of overseas students in many universities in many countries. In Australia the proportion of international students had risen by 2019 to approximately 25% of all university new enrolments, higher than in the UK and much higher than in the USA. This creates a massive financial risk to the future sustainability of the university sector, as has been demonstrated by the Covid-19 pandemic. At the time of writing, universities in Australia, as well as in the UK and probably elsewhere, are laying off staff and are facing an uncertain future due to this sudden income reduction. Elsewhere I discuss the impact on research funding.

Assuming that the 'trade' in overseas students does resume, we need to explore previous concerns about the impact of a high proportion of overseas students. Does it reduce the learning experience of other students, does it lead to the exclusion of local students, or does the income allow for an increase in educational resources (buildings and staff for example) with flow-on for local educational needs.

Do overseas student crowd out local students?

Let's summarise the extent of overseas student involvement in local universities—and I will use Australia as my main point of reference. From 2002 to 2019, there was an almost fourfold increase in overseas student numbers in higher education in Australia (International student enrolments in Australia 1994–2019). This represents around a quarter of all university students, and around 40% of students in the 'Group of Eight' most prestigious universities. The largest number came from China. By

2017, this represented 23% of all operating revenue—over 30% in the Group of Eight.

Babones in his 2019 paper 'The China Student Boom and the Risks it Poses to Australian Universities' (Babones 2019) emphasises the large dependence on overseas students from China. He has explored the situation in seven of the Group of Eight universities, where around half of the overseas students are from China and alerts that *"International comparisons reveal the excessiveness of this China exposure. All seven have higher proportions of international and Chinese students than any university in the entire United States. Indeed, all seven appear to be more dependent on fee-paying Chinese students than just about any other universities in the English-speaking world."* He concludes: *"Australia's universities are taking a multi-billion dollar gamble with taxpayer money to pursue a high-risk, high-reward international growth strategy that may ultimately prove incompatible with their public service mission. Their revenues have boomed as they enrol record numbers of international students, particularly from China. As long as their bets on the international student market pay off, the universities' gamble will look like a success. If their bets go sour, taxpayers may be called on to help pick up the tab."* As overseas student numbers plummet in response to the Covid-19 pandemic, his fears have come to pass.

Birrell (2019) points out that among the Group of Eight universities (Go8), in the 5 years to 2017, domestic enrolments were static and all the increase was in overseas student numbers *"Clearly, the Go8 universities preferred to enrol overseas students. In effect, the benefits of the allegedly superior education that these universities offer went to overseas students rather than to local students. This was not because overseas students had superior potential to take advantage of what the Go8 offers. The contrary is the case. The Go8 do not preference high performing overseas students. There are minimal entry barriers to their enrolment other than the ability to pay the huge fees required."*

There are other indirect financial gains for the population from the large number of overseas student consuming various commodities (housing, food, travel etc.), leading to overseas students representing Australia's third largest export earner, behind iron ore and coal. As Birrell also tells us, this is a direct result of government policy to encourage this trend.

Do overseas students lead to a reduction in educational outcomes or standards?

Foster (2012) has found that *"Adding international or domestic non-English speaking background (NESB) students to a tutorial classroom leads to a reduction in most students' marks, and there is a particularly strong negative association between international NESB student concentrations in tutorial classrooms and the marks of students from English-speaking backgrounds"*. Controversially, she also finds: *"the impact on marks of a high percentage of NESB students in a course is positive"* but suggests that this may be due to *"…influences such as downward adjustments to the difficulty of material or grading standards."* In which case this would compound the problem.

Birrell and Betts (2018) comment that there has been a reduction in teaching standards, partly to accommodate limited preparation and lower language skills of overseas students. In relation to the Group of Eight universities *"Teaching is a second order priority. Students hoping to get the benefits of exposure to top researchers find instead that teaching is regarded as a chore or a distraction by the research stars. Most face-to-face teaching is conducted by non-tenured adjuncts."*

According to Babones: *"Australian universities routinely compromise admissions standards to accommodate international students. Preparatory programs for students with lower English language test scores function as a paid work-around for international students who do not meet admissions standards. By prominently marketing such alternative pathways, Australian universities are in effect taking actions that reduce their financial risks by increasing their standards risks."*

Babones further states: *"Much of the growth in international student numbers at the seven focus universities has been directed into business education. The five for which data are available draw more than 40% of their entire business student bodies from overseas; for Melbourne and Sydney universities, the figure is 66.9%."* Whether this denies local students access to business studies, or actually increases their access since there are now nice buildings and excellent teachers employed from the fee income is not clear and was not studied, but he does conclude that: *"Instead of focusing on providing a high quality education and upskilling Australia's population, the universities sector has become focussed on pushing through as many students as possible in order to maximise fees and profit"*.

Of course the universities themselves have a different view on the role of international students, and I have not quoted their side of the story. A press release from the Deputy Chief Executive of Universities Australia in 2018 says (Media Release 2018): *"International education is a modern Australian success story – built from the ground up over six decades to become the nation's third-largest export and the envy of the world."* The press release does not touch on educational standards, and the university sector will dispute any reduction in standards by overseas students. Following the Covid-19 induced damage to the sector, I think that a press release today might tell a different story.

The theme I am building of the need for a radical re-think of how to provide university education for the future, must include a reduction in reliance on overseas student fees. The next section shows how this, and the underlying problem of the underlying university business model, has a pernicious effect on global educational needs.

2.6 Global Inequalities in Educational Need are Ignored

My experience at both universities of Newcastle and Manchester gave me exposure to issues of the global inequalities in access to education. From Newcastle I travelled extensively across the developing world, and met educators and students in many settings as well as a number of academics and organisations involved in global health research and development. The commitment of all of these people and organisations towards reducing inequalities in access to education was remarkable and empowering.

At the same time, universities were building greater reliance on overseas student fee income. I have a couple of personal examples of how financial gain has hindered global access to education. The first was at the University of Newcastle, when fees for overseas students came in and I argued for low fees for our students from developing countries on our Public Health courses so as to make them more available in low-income settings. I was over ruled by the Vice-Chancellor who said that a low fee would send a signal that the course was low quality and high fees indicated high quality. The other story is from the University of Manchester, where I had set up its first fully online master's degree and managed to keep costs for overseas students affordable so that we could offer this course on Public Health to those who really need it to help their poor populations with major health problems. As soon as I retired, the School accountant doubled the fees for overseas students—as I mentioned in the introduction to this book, it was this experience that led me to develop the Peoples-uni to provide this type of education at low cost.

Of course there is more to it than the financial needs of universities in high income countries. There are global inequalities in access to higher education both within countries and between countries. Despite the observation that access to higher education has increased steadily over recent years, the increase is much greater in high than low-income countries as shown in Fig. 2.3 from a UNESCO report (Policy Paper 2017).

The same UNESCO report (Policy Paper 2017) tells us that the rate of access to higher education among those in the 5 years when access might be expected, following the age of high school completion, varies from less than 1% in the poorest group in the poorest countries to more than 70% in the richest group in the richest countries (Fig. 2.4).

Within a number of countries there are initiatives to widen access to higher education so that it is available to all sectors of society. In a study of 71 countries across all continents, Salmi (2018) found that despite equity of access being an important priority in all countries surveyed, *"only 32% of the countries have defined specific participation targets for any equity group, and only 11% of the countries surveyed have formulated a comprehensive equity strategy. Another 11% have elaborated a specific policy document for one equity group, gender, people with disabilities, or members of indigenous groups."* Despite 'headline' national priorities, action to widen participation appears to be limited.

But what is the role of the university in helping to reduce inequalities between nations? Is this an appropriate role for the university sector? If so, is global education being offered with the real aim of reducing these inequalities, or rather helping to support their own university sector? I have previously mentioned that the large and continuing grant that my University received from the Rockefeller Foundation arguably helped us as much as the intended recipients—we employed more staff and were able to provide education for more Australians than for overseas students. Although the programme was aimed at building education and research capacity in

2.6 Global Inequalities in Educational Need are Ignored

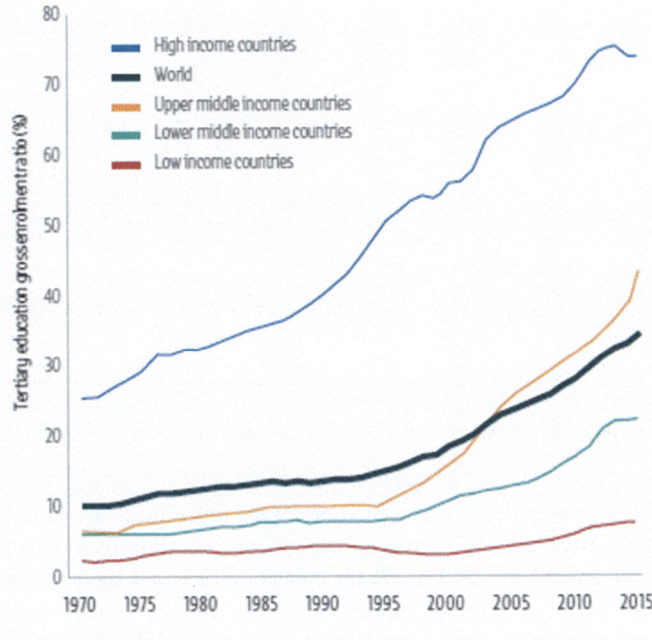

Fig. 2.3 Growth in tertiary education over time by country income group (UNESCO)

developing countries, and has led to long-term teaching and research capacity development, as much capacity was created at our university as in any of the individual target universities in developing countries.

Of course the education sector is not the only one where international aid creates benefit 'back home'. A study of the Australian overseas aid sector found that one dollar of aid increased Australian exports by more than seven dollars (Otor and Dornan 2017).

We have already discussed the importance to the university sector, and the national economies, at least Australia and the UK, of the fees obtained from overseas students. This has been brought into sharp focus by the Covid-19 pandemic with its travel restrictions which have threatened the viability of a number of universities in Australia which were over-reliant on this income source.

Many western country universities have established campuses in developing countries—and some have become bankrupt due the inappropriateness of the business model. What was the rationale of the establishment of these campuses—financial gain for the university or capacity building in the overseas country?

Vast differences exist in higher attainment between the poor and the rich
Percentage of 25-29 year olds who have completed at least four years of tertiary education, by wealth, selected countries, 2008–2014

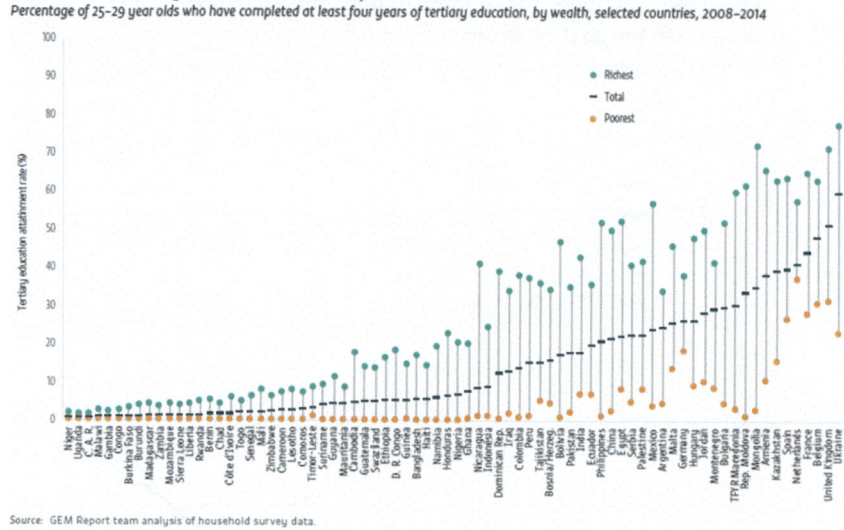

Source: GEM Report team analysis of household survey data.

Fig. 2.4 Inequalities in completing higher education within and between countries (UNESCO)

So whose responsibility is it to try to correct the imbalance? We have previously discussed that universities now see their responsibilities primarily as businesses, and secondarily as serving national needs for education. It is not their role to consider global issues of educational requirements, even if many individual academics have that concern. Individual governments should take responsibility for the education of their population, although economic constraints may restrict this ability. No international organisation really has a global oversight, in the way that the World Health Organisation has for global health with a goal *'to ensure that a billion more people have universal health coverage, to protect a billion more people from health emergencies, and provide a further billion people with better health and well-being'*. UNESCO *'seeks to build peace through international cooperation in Education...'* which is much less action oriented. Various non-governmental organisations aim to improve global educational outcomes, particularly for primary school and gender equality in educational access. The Global Partnership for Education https://www.globalpartnership.org/ *'mobilizes investments, both external and domestic, to help governments build stronger education systems, based on data and evidence'* and *'has mobilized more than US$7 billion for education, creating better opportunities for millions of children, their communities and their countries.'* The Sustainable Development Goals include education in SDG4 to *'Ensure inclusive and equitable quality education and promote lifelong learning opportunities for all'* and the SDG target 4.3 states: *'By 2030, ensure equal access for all women and men to affordable and quality technical, vocational and tertiary education, including university'*.

Despite the creation of a global target, there seems to be no body that takes an action oriented approach to reducing global inequalities in higher education.

2.6 Global Inequalities in Educational Need are Ignored

Hill and Lawton (2018) state that achieving the SDG4 goal "*...will require a monumental reversal of higher education being placed in the service of national goals based on competitive advantage*" and that "*Moral responsibility in tackling inequality is less clear at international level, not only because it would require a heroic level of international coordination, but because it is inconsistent with national policy goals*". Going further, they suggest: "*In spite of far-reaching international teaching partnerships and international cooperation in research, higher education is hard-wired to the pursuit of economic nationalism. For those who believe that growing inequality is a problem worth tackling, this is the opposite of what the world needs from higher education.*"

Marginson (2018) makes a similar point about global research "*In the absence of a global state or regulatory framework, issues of under-production and under-funding of global common goods cannot be fully addressed. Who funds global common goods?*".

There are a number of partnerships between university research groups across the global divide, clearly aimed at boosting local research capacity in developing countries—although Baker (2020) voices concerns that most of the publications resulting from these collaborations are driven by the developed country partner with very little research leadership arising in the developing country partner. "*LDCs' (Less Developed Countries) productivity is significantly boosted by the effect of international collaboration. In 2018, about 15,000 of the 21,000 papers they produced involved cross-border collaboration.*"

Baker points to the UK's Independent Commission for Aid Impact review of the Newton Fund (https://icai.independent.gov.uk/review/newton-fund/) which found "*The Newton Fund is a research and innovation partnership fund managed by the Department for Business, Energy and Industrial Strategy (BEIS), which was established to develop science and innovation partnerships to reduce poverty by generating and putting into use knowledge and technology, with a secondary purpose to strengthen the UK's wider prosperity and global influence....However, the fund was poorly designed to pursue the aim of promoting international development, and in reality its secondary objectives – such as building ties with partner countries like China, India, Brazil and South Africa – have often been the main driver of its work. An estimated 90% of UK aid spent through the Newton Fund stays in the UK with UK institutions, which is contrary, at least in spirit, to the UK government's commitment to untying all UK aid.*" This seems consistent with my anecdote about my experience with my University's grant from the Rockefeller Foundation.

A dated but relevant book Global Inequalities and Higher Education by Unterhalter and Carpentier (2010) explores many of these issues also, and tries to identify "*whose interests do higher education institutions serve?*" Unterhalter (2017) further comments: "*Inequality in higher education capabilities for institutions and individuals tends to undermine investigation into global public goods. That such questions of global public good are ignored has something to do with the way global inequalities in higher education are taken for granted. Naming these inequalities and questioning their foundations is an important project.*"

While my personal experience and many of the publications refer to the situation in the UK and Australia, there are some countries, particularly in Scandinavia, where the universities are really able to focus on real needs in reducing global inequality.

My conclusion is that universities, despite the best intentions of individual educators and researchers, are ill equipped to contribute to reducing global inequalities in education and research capacity, as they respond to their own funding needs and the economic and educational nationalism of their countries. Some kind of global solution is required—and I have made some suggestions later on in this book.

Moving away from the problems of the business imperative that drives universities and the structural and organisational themes I have been discussing, there is a fundamental problem in the way that education is provided to young people. Universities are taking too long to adapt their teaching to the way that young people learn today, as outlined in the next section.

2.7 Universities have Not Kept Up with the Way Young People Gain Information

Much of my personal teaching experience has revolved around individual mentoring or small group teaching. As a clinical teacher I would have small group discussions around an individual patient to identify disease diagnosis and treatment with a focus on the evidence base for both. As a 'lecturer' I would run small group seminars and as an academic supervisor I would mentor individuals as they pursued their own research towards a higher degree. I really dislike both giving and attending lectures. At the University of Manchester, I was lucky to have a junior lecturer in my team who liked being on the stage and she very kindly took most of my lecturing duties. When in the audience, I am also usually very shy about asking questions at the end of lecture. Yet I spend a large part of my day, every day, asking questions to find information that I want or need in a different way—by interrogating the internet. And I did not grow up with the internet.

A few years ago, I was asked to evaluate the teaching programme in a major university in another country, and found that they were giving lectures to 500 students at a time. The students did not like them, nor did the academic staff, but my recommendation to replace lectures with alternative methods was ignored by the administration—their use was said to be 'cost-effective'. Not very costly maybe, but effective?

Lectures, the 'sage on the stage' approach, have been the main educational method throughout the history of universities—their academics are called 'lecturers' for a good reason. This is a form of passive learning, and has been acknowledged as a poor way of transmitting information for a long time. Alternative educational methods through creating active learning opportunities have been introduced in many settings. The results of a meta-analysis of 225 studies of student performance in science, engineering, and mathematics indicate that average examination scores improved by about 6% in active learning environments, and that students in classes with traditional lecturing were 1.5 times more likely to fail than were students in classes with active learning (Freeman et al. 2014). The authors make the point that if such a high failure rate had been found in a randomised controlled trial of a medical intervention, the trial would have been stopped and those in the lecturing arm transferred to active learning for ethical reasons! The authors also state that their results are quite similar to other published studies in the educational literature.

Schmidt and colleagues (2015) think that the problem with lectures is the 'information transmission fallacy'—people need to do something with the knowledge they are given rather than just receive it if they are to remember and use it in the future. Hence various opportunities for active learning, such as problem based learning where students work together to solve a problem, are alternatives to the lecture.

A broader issue than the way that lecturers transmit information, and less frequently discussed, is whether the lecturer is needed or not—is self-based learning not as good as, or better than, the tutor? There are many examples today and historically of autodidacts, who teach themselves and have successful careers based on what they have learned. I don't want to extend this discussion to school based teaching, and I do appreciate the importance of having role models amongst our teachers, but there are some relevant data. In a study of mine (Heller et al. 2019), we ran a couple of online courses for continuing professional development with and without tutor support, and showed no difference in outcome (course completion and grades) between tutor-led and tutor-free options. There are other examples, although not many good trials in the literature. I'm setting the scene for a discussion on the potential for online learning, and as you will see this fits in with many of the other themes I have developed so far.

A 2017 national study of American medical students (Nadell 2018) found that less than half of them reported attending classes or lectures in person 'Most of the time' or 'Often' and nearly a quarter said 'Almost never'. The anecdotal literature is full of similar lack of attendance at university classes. So where can students gain information? The internet is today's answer due to the speed of access, breadth of educational materials available, and the increasing availability of access.

As with all sectors of the global population, young people are accessing the internet in increasing numbers. Teenagers use the internet for various reasons, including finding information especially to help with school projects as schools increasingly use the internet as part of their educational processes. Stimulated by the global Covid-19 pandemic, school classes have been offered online. Young people entering universities have been used to gain their information from the internet, so they are primed for this methods of learning, not for lectures.

The Internet Society (Internet Society. Internet Access and Education 2017) unsurprisingly claims that the internet has great potential to improve education quality, and to contribute to global sustainable development.

I don't think that it is news that the internet is becoming increasingly available and accessed. As the picture below, taken from the Pew Foundation for US data (Pew Research Center 2017), shows, this does vary by age, with very high rates in young people (Fig. 2.5).

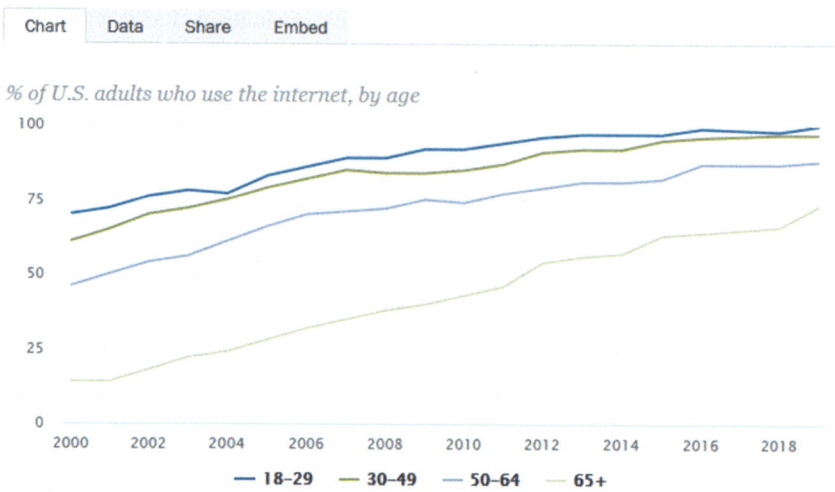

Fig. 2.5 Internet use by age in the US

The age gradient is also seen in Africa, again from the Pew Foundation (Silver and Johnson 2018), where rates are still lower than in other parts of the world, but growing (Fig. 2.6).

There is also a social gradient in internet use, as shown in this figure from the same Pew Foundation survey in Africa where the more educated are more likely to use the internet than the less educated (Fig. 2.7).

This digital divide does pose a problem for relying too much on internet use for education, as it runs the risk of increasing the educational divide within populations. There appears to be an increasing gender gap in digital development, and the majority of those without internet are in the developing world (International Telecommunication Union 2019). A report in the New York Times quotes students in Indonesia who have to climb trees to get a phone signal to allow them to submit their assignments, and that a third of students have limited or no internet access (Paddock and Sijabat 2020). However, over time there have been substantial global increases in access to the internet, and this will undoubtedly improve further over time.

The Pew Research Centre survey (Silver and Johnson 2018) also reports that Sub-Saharan Africans feel that the internet has already had a considerable positive impact on education.

Selwyn (2013) puts it nicely: "..*online practices have been part of young people's lives since birth and, much like oxygen, water, or electricity, are assumed to be a basic condition of modern life....For many commentators, the Internet has always been an inherently educational tool. Indeed, many people would argue that the main characteristics of the Internet align closely with the core concerns of education. For instance, both the Internet* and *education are concerned with information exchange,*

2.7 Universities have Not Kept Up with the Way Young …

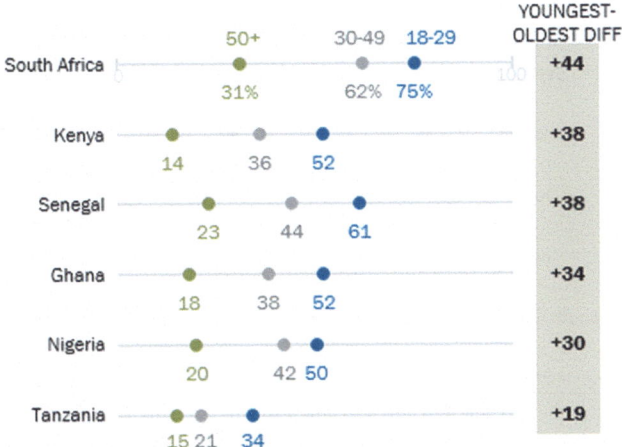

Fig. 2.6 Internet use by age in Sub-Saharan Africa

communication, and the creation of knowledge." Selwyn also lists many potential educational advantages of internet based learning over the more traditional methods.

The acknowledged deficiencies in much of the way that universities do their teaching, the knowledge that young people gain their information online these days, and the potential educational advantages of online education provide a wonderful opportunity to re-cast university educational processes.

The final section in my problems list is probably the most fundamental—that universities' structure and educational methods are not sustainable in this era of climate change.

2.8 Environmental Sustainability is Ignored

It was while working in Newcastle that I attended a conference and went for a run with a colleague on the beach (Australian Public Health conference organisers are no strangers to finding venues that might attract an audience). I asked my colleague if there was any substance to the developing concerns about global warming. He gave me a short (breathless) tutorial about not only the reality and causes of climate

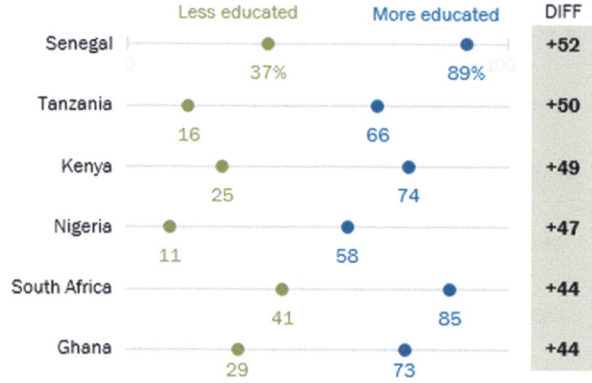

Fig. 2.7 Internet use by education in sub-Saharan Africa

change, but also the health effects. He later went on to become one of the leaders in that academic field.

My personal interest in the environmental effects of climate change evolved slowly. Looking back, my frequent flights between Australia and other countries as part of my work in global health capacity building were an embarrassingly high source of carbon emissions. When I was working at the University of Manchester, as part of the extensive campus building programme an avenue of lovely old trees was cut down. I complained to the Vice-Chancellor and received the reply that when trees were to be cut down, they would be replaced somewhere else on the campus by new trees. I retired before following up to see if the promise had been kept, but of course this was only a very small part of the issue of the relation between universities and environmental sustainability. More important, and much more relevant to my personal experience, is the development of distance and open learning initiatives with which I have been involved throughout my career in the Universities of Newcastle and Manchester, and the International Clinical Epidemiology Network and Peoples-uni. Online delivery of education has the major added benefit of being much more environmentally sustainable than face-to-face education.

There is currently a very active discussion across the higher education sector about environmental sustainability. Universities have a potentially important role in

2.8 Environmental Sustainability is Ignored

both ensuring that their own practices are environmentally sustainable and offering education and performing research into the issues. As Leal Filho and colleagues (2015) pointed out back in 2015 "*At present, many higher education institutions are becoming more aware of their impact on the environment, and trying to understand the environmental needs and implications of their operations. Going further, some universities are incorporating sustainability principles into their activities. One of the questions that universities are now facing is how education for sustainable development can be translated into practice so that it can be effective in transforming society.*" How far have universities incorporated sustainability issues in the curriculum across faculties and disciplines?

Here are some pictures of beautiful new university buildings in or near Sydney. One designed by a globally famous 'starchitect'. Go inside and they are full of light and space, a wonderful environment in which to study. We have previously discussed how the high number of overseas students are funding university infrastructure—none more than for business schools. What is the impact on the environment of these wonderful buildings? (Figs. 2.8, 2.9 and 2.10)

At the global level, Sustainable Development Goals are the '*blueprint to achieve a better and more sustainable future for all*' (https://sustainabledevelopment.un.org/sdgs). Adopted by all United Nations Member States in 2015, the 2030 Agenda for Sustainable Development provides '*a shared blueprint for peace and prosperity*

Fig. 2.8 University of Sydney Business School

Fig. 2.9 University of Technology Sydney Business School

for people and the planet, now and into the future. The 17 Sustainable Development Goals (SDGs), which are an urgent call for action by all countries - developed and developing - in a global partnership. They recognize that ending poverty and other deprivations must go hand-in-hand with strategies that improve health and education, reduce inequality, and spur economic growth – all while tackling climate change and working to preserve our oceans and forests'. There is a 'Sustainable Development Goal Accord' (https://www.sdgaccord.org/), supported by the Higher Education Sustainability Initiative (https://sustainabledevelopment.un.org/sdinaction/hesi), which is the higher education sector's response, and which has identified five core areas of how educational institutions can engage with the Sustainable Development Goals with a specific focus on SDG 4 (Quality Education), SDG 8 (Decent Work and Economic Growth) and SDG 17 (Partnership for the Goals):

(1) Teaching sustainable development across all disciplines of study, including through online based platforms,
(2) Encouraging research and dissemination of sustainable development knowledge,
(3) Green campuses and supporting local sustainability efforts,
(4) Engaging and share information with and through international networks,
(5) Engaging universities in local and national government, as well as city development projects.

Institutions and individuals are encouraged to sign the Accord, and it is clear that these 5 core areas of work may make a contribution. It remains to be seen how actively the higher education sector actually embraces these activities. The global

2.8 Environmental Sustainability is Ignored

Fig. 2.10 University of Newcastle, New South Wales, City Campus

sustainability agenda is very large, and the higher education sector has a role in it, unfortunately none of the 5 core areas above cover what I really want to discuss.

My focus here is more fundamentally on the impact on the environment of the way universities are established and offer their education. When you base the educational experience on face-to-face contacts between staff and students, such as in lectures, you do need buildings. I want to suggest a system change to mainly online learning. I will present my prescription for a distributed university in the 'solutions' chapter of the book.

Bringing people into a physical learning environment involves travel by students and staff, as well as making sure you have the buildings to house them. All of these have an environmental impact. This is magnified for overseas students. In a paper that my colleagues and I have submitted for publication, we explore the environmental impact savings of online education. A cohort of 128 students enrolled in the Manchester Metropolitan University's Master of Public Health which was actually taught by Peoples-uni fully online (more on Peoples-uni in other chapters). Students came from 31 countries and we estimate that learning online in their home environments rather than travelling to and living in Manchester saved nearly a million kilograms of CO_2. Imagine the savings from a general pivot from face-to-face to online education.

I like this from Warden (Warden 2020) reporting a presentation by Tilbury *"Rethinking not tinkering...Rather than adding on, what is needed is a total overhaul"*.

It is a total re-thinking of education which I am also proposing. The various sections so far seem to have a common theme—that there is a need for re-thinking higher education, In the next chapter of the book we will see how each of the areas discussed might be dealt with in a new system.

References

Aspromourgos, T. The managerialist university: An economic interpretation [online]. Australian Universities' Review 2012;54:44–9. https://search.informit.org/doi/10.3316/INFORMIT.754829907409031.

Babones S. The China student boom and the risks it poses to Australian Universities. CIS Analysis Paper 5, Sydney, Centre for Independent Studies, August 2019.

Baker S. Are research links with the developing world still a one-way street? Times Higher Education, January 2020. https://www.timeshighereducation.com/features/are-research-links-developing-world-still-one-way-street.

Bennett D, Roberts L, Ananthram S. Teaching-only roles could mark the end of your academic career. The Conversation, March 2017. https://theconversation.com/teaching-only-roles-could-mark-the-end-of-your-academic-career-74826.

Birrell B. Overseas students are driving Australia's net overseas migration tide. The Australian Population Research Institute; April 2019. https://apo.org.au/node/232056.

Birrell B, Betts K. Australia's higher education overseas student industry revisited. The Australian Population Research Institute, Research Report, December 2018. https://apo.org.au/node/215036.

Burnes B, Wend P, By RT. The changing face of English universities: reinventing collegiality for the twenty-first century. Stud High Educ. 2014;39(6):905–26. https://doi.org/10.1080/03075079.2012.754858.

Chalmers D. Recognising and rewarding teaching: Australian teaching criteria and standards and expert peer review Final report: April 2019. ISBN 978-1-76051-667-3 Australian Department of Education and Training.

Craig R, Amernic J, Tourish D. Perverse audit culture and accountability of the modern public university. Financ Accountability Manage. 2014;30:1–24. https://doi.org/10.1111/faam.12025.

Davies B. Death to critique and dissent? The policies and practices of new managerialism and of 'Evidence-based Practice'. Gender Educ. 2003;15.

Deem R. 'New managerialism' and higher education: The management of performances and cultures in universities in the United Kingdom. Int Stud Sociol Educ. 1998;8(1):47–70. https://doi.org/10.1080/0962021980020014.

Deem R, Brehony KJ. Management as ideology: the case of 'new managerialism' in higher education. Oxf Rev Educ. 2005;31(2):217–35. https://doi.org/10.1080/03054980500117827.

Erickson M, Hanna P, Walker C. The UK higher education senior management survey: a statactivist response to managerialist governance. Studies in Higher Education; 2020 (online). https://doi.org/10.1080/03075079.2020.1712693.

References

Figlio D, Schapiro MO. Are great teachers poor scholars? Brookings Institute, January 2017. https://www.brookings.edu/research/are-great-teachers-poor-scholars/.

Foster G. The impact of international students on measured learning and standards in Australian higher education; 2012. https://www.sciencedirect.com/science/article/abs/pii/S0272775712000283.

Freeman S, Eddy SL, McDonough M, Smith MK, Okoroafor N, Jordt H, Wenderoth MP. Active learning increases student performance in science, engineering, and mathematics. Proc Natl Acad Sci. 2014;111(23):8410–5. https://doi.org/10.1073/pnas.1319030111.

Graeber D. Bullshit jobs. The rise of pointless work, and what we can do about it. Penguin Press; 2019.

Halffman W, Radder H. The academic manifesto: from an occupied to a Public University. Minerva. 2015;53:165–87. https://doi.org/10.1007/s11024-015-9270-9.

Heller R, Chilolo E, Elliott J, Johnson B, Lipman D, Ononeze V, Richards J. Do tutors make a difference in online learning? A comparative study in two Open Online Courses. Open Praxis. 2019;11:229–41. https://openpraxis.org/articles/10.5944/openpraxis.11.3.960/.

Hill C, Lawton W. Universities, the digital divide and global inequality. J High Educ Policy Manag. 2018;40:598–610. https://doi.org/10.1080/1360080X.2018.1531211.

Hiltzik M. Column: When universities try to behave like businesses, education suffers. LA Times, June 2016. https://www.latimes.com/business/hiltzik/la-fi-hiltzik-university-business-20160602-snap-story.html.

Independent Commission for Aid Impact. The Newton Fund. https://icai.independent.gov.uk/report/newton-fund/.

International student enrolments in Australia 1994–2019. Australian Government, Department of Education, Skills and Employment; 2019. https://internationaleducation.gov.au/research/International-Student-Data/Pages/InternationalStudentData2019.aspx.

International students inject $32 billion a year into Australia's economy—boosting Aussie jobs and wages. Universities Australia. Media release, August 2018. https://www.universitiesaustralia.edu.au/media-item/international-students-inject-32-billion-a-year-into-australias-economy-boosting-aussie-jobs-and-wages/.

International Telecommunication Union (ITU). Facts and figures 2019: Measuring digital development. https://itu.foleon.com/itu/measuring-digital-development/home/.

Internet Society. Internet Access and Education: Key considerations for policy makers. November 2017. https://www.internetsociety.org/resources/doc/2017/internet-access-and-education/.

Keashly L, Neuman JH. Faculty experiences with bullying in higher education. Adm Theor Praxis. 2015;32(1):48–70. https://doi.org/10.2753/ATP1084-1806320103.

Kellermann P. The university as a business?. In: Rondo-Brovetto P, Saliterer I, editors. The university as a business. Springer Science & Business Media; 2011.

Koens L, Hofman R, de Jonge J. What motivates researchers? Research excellence is still a priority. The Hague: Rathenau Instituut; 2018. https://www.rathenau.nl/en/vitale-kennisecosystemen/what-motivates-researchers.

Leal Filho W, Shiel C, do Paço A (2015) Integrative approaches to environmental sustainability at universities: an overview of challenges and priorities. J Integr Environ Sci. 2015;12:1–14. https://doi.org/10.1080/1943815X.2014.988273.

Marginson S. Dynamics of national and global competition in higher education. High Educ. 2006;52:1–39. https://doi.org/10.1007/s10734-004-7649-x.

Marginson S. The new geo-politics of higher education. Centre for Global Higher Education working paper series. Working paper number 34, April 2018.

Mathews D: If you love research, academia may not be for you. Times Higher Education, November 2018. https://www.timeshighereducation.com/blog/if-you-love-research-academia-may-not-be-you.

McKenna S. Here are five signs that universities are turning into corporations. The Conversation, March 2018. https://theconversation.com/here-are-five-signs-that-universities-are-turning-into-corporations-93100.

Media Release. International students inject $32 billion a year into Australia's economy—boosting Aussie jobs and wages. Universities Australia, August 2018. https://www.universitiesaustralia.edu.au/media-item/international-students-inject-32-billion-a-year-into-australias-economy-boosting-aussie-jobs-and-wages/.

Musselin C. New forms of competition in higher education. Soc Econ Rev. 2018;16:657–83. https://doi.org/10.1093/ser/mwy033.

Nadell Farber O. Medical students are skipping class in droves—and making lectures increasingly obsolete. August 2018. https://www.statnews.com/2018/08/14/medical-students-skipping-class/.

Naidoo R. Competition as a fetish: why universities need to escape the trap. The Conversation, April 2016. https://theconversation.com/competition-as-a-fetish-why-universities-need-to-escape-the-trap-58084.

Norton A. Is university research good for teaching? The Conversation, July 2013. http://theconversation.com/is-university-research-good-for-teaching-16225.

Norton A, Sonnemann J. Cherastidtham I. Taking university teaching seriously. Grattan Institute; 2013. ISBN: 978-1-925015-42-3.

Orr Y, Orr R. The death of Socrates: Managerialism, metrics and bureaucratisation in universities. Australian Universities' Rev. 2016;58:15–5. https://www.nteu.org.au/qute/article/The-Death-of-Socrates%3A-Managerialism%2C-metrics-and-bureaucratisation-in-universities-%28AUR-58-02%29-18949.

Otor S, Dornan M. How does foreign aid impact Australian exports in the long-run? Development Policy Centre Discussion Paper #62, Crawford School of Public Policy, The Australian National University, Canberra; 2017.

Rose, NS. Powers of Freedom. Cambridge University Press, 1999.

Paddock RC, Sijabat DM. When learning is really remote: students climb trees and travel miles for a cell signal. New York Times, September 2020. https://www.nytimes.com/2020/09/05/world/asia/coronavirus-indonesia-school-remote-learning.html.

Palali A, Elk R, Bolhaar J, Rud I. Are good researchers also good teachers? The relationship between research quality and teaching quality. Econ Educ Rev. 2018;64:40–9. https://doi.org/10.1016/j.econedurev.2018.03.011.

Pelizzon A, Young M, Joannes-Boyau R. 'Universities are not corporations': 600 Australian academics call for change to uni governance structures. The Conversation, July 2020. https://theconversation.com/universities-are-not-corporations-600-australian-academics-call-for-change-to-uni-governance-structures-143254.

Pew Research Center. Internet use by age. January 2017. https://www.pewresearch.org/internet/chart/internet-use-by-age/.

Policy Paper April 2017 Six ways to ensure higher education leaves no one behind UNESCO IIEP [3383] Document code: ED/GEMR/MRT/2017/PP/30. https://unesdoc.unesco.org/ark:/48223/pf0000247862.

Salin D. Ways of explaining workplace bullying: a review of enabling, motivating, and precipitating structures and processes in the work environment. Human Relat. 2003;56:1213–32. https://doi.org/10.1177/00187267035610003.

Salmi J. All around the world—Higher education equity policies across the globe. Lumina Foundation, November 2018

Schmidt HG, Wagener SL, Smeets GACM, Keemink LM, van der Molen HT. On the use and misuse of lectures in higher education. Health Professions Educ. 2015;1:12–8. https://doi.org/10.1016/j.hpe.2015.11.010.

Scott P. Universities are losing their sense of public responsibility and social purpose. The Guardian, January 2015. https://www.theguardian.com/education/2015/jan/06/public-universities-becoming-corporate-losing-social-purpose.

Selwyn N. The internet and education; 2013. https://www.bbvaopenmind.com/en/articles/the-internet-and-education/.

Shepherd S. Managerialism: an ideal type. Stud High Educ. 2018;43:1668–78. https://doi.org/10.1080/03075079.2017.1281239.

References

Silver S, Johnson C. Internet use is growing across much of sub-Saharan Africa, but most are still offline. Pew Research Center, October 2018. https://www.pewresearch.org/global/2018/10/09/internet-use-is-growing-across-much-of-sub-saharan-africa-but-most-are-still-offline/.

Silver S, Johnson C. Sub-Saharan Africans say internet use has positively impacted education, personal relationships and economy. Pew Research Center, October 2018. https://www.pewresearch.org/global/2018/10/09/sub-saharan-africans-say-internet-use-has-positively-impacted-education-personal-relationships-and-economy/.

Skinner T, Peez D, Strachan G, Whitehouse G, Bailey J, Broadbent K. Self-reported harassment and bullying in Australian universities: explaining differences between regional, metropolitan and elite institutions. J High Educ Policy Manag. 2015;37:558–71. https://doi.org/10.1080/1360080X.2015.1079400.

Sustainable Development Goals. https://sustainabledevelopment.un.org/sdgs.

Sustainable Development Goal (SDG) Accord. https://www.sdgaccord.org/.

The Higher Education Sustainability Initiative https://sustainabledevelopment.un.org/sdinaction/hesi.

Unterhalter E. Global: What is wrong with global inequality in higher education?. In: Mihut G, Altbach PG, Wit H, editors. Understanding global higher education. Global perspectives on higher education. Rotterdam: SensePublishers; 2017.

Unterhalter E, Carpentier V. Global inequalities and higher education. Palgrave Macmillam; 2010. ISBN: 9780230223516.

Warden R. Sustainable development: Are universities ready to lead? University World News, March 2020. https://www.universityworldnews.com/post.php?story=20200310143004253.

West D. The systemic pathologies of university 'managerialism'. Sydney Morning Herald; 2015. https://www.smh.com.au/opinion/the-systemic-pathologies-of-university-managerialism-20151030-gkmoti.html.

Whitehead M, Orton L, Nayak S, Petticrew M, Sowden A White M. How could differences in 'control over destiny' lead to socio-economic inequalities in health? A synthesis of theories and pathways in the living environment. Health Place 2016;39:51–1. https://doi.org/10.1016/j.healthplace.2016.02.002.

Zaglas W. Murdoch University's 'aggressive' student recruitment could hurt other Australian universities. Campus Review, October 2019. https://www.campusreview.com.au/2019/10/murdoch-universitys-aggressive-student-recruitment-could-hurt-other-australian-universities/.

Open Access This chapter is licensed under the terms of the Creative Commons Attribution 4.0 International License (http://creativecommons.org/licenses/by/4.0/), which permits use, sharing, adaptation, distribution and reproduction in any medium or format, as long as you give appropriate credit to the original author(s) and the source, provide a link to the Creative Commons license and indicate if changes were made.

The images or other third party material in this chapter are included in the chapter's Creative Commons license, unless indicated otherwise in a credit line to the material. If material is not included in the chapter's Creative Commons license and your intended use is not permitted by statutory regulation or exceeds the permitted use, you will need to obtain permission directly from the copyright holder.

Chapter 3
Solutions

Abstract Universities should develop a system of trust in academic staff to replace managerialism, replace competition with collaboration, and adopt a global perspective to educational inequalities. Three new programmes are proposed. Universities should place education in a framework of environmental sustainability—the Distributed University, moving to online learning which will become the main mode of university education in the future.

Keywords Managerialism · Collaboration · Online learning · Environmental sustainability

Building on the identification of problems in the previous chapter, I now turn to solutions. I hope that you will appreciate the progression from problem to solution. I am suggesting that trust replace managerialism, that collaboration replace the competition of commercialisation, that we use online learning as the key educational mode to reflect the way young people learn, that we share educational resources, and that we take a global perspective to educational inequalities. These will all place education in the context of environmental sustainability, using a distributed university structure. I have a number of detailed programmatic suggestions—a higher educational variant of the International Baccalaureate, a 'Global Online Learning' programme, and a 'Plan E for Education' to increase public access to higher education. An ambitious set of suggestions, I know. But we do need ambition and innovation for the university sector to survive and prosper.

3.1 Develop Trust in Academic Staff to Replace Managerialism

I described in the section on managerialism how my personal autonomy to administer a large grant was eroded by university managers. Initially I was trusted to administer my own group to meet the requirements of the grant I led, as well as for the other grants received, but this was removed as part of an institutional reorganisation. The section also described how managerialism has interfered with many academic activities such as approval of courses and assessments and any university academic today can give many more personal examples where managerialism has added to workload by creating extra internal regulatory requirements, and diminished a sense of academic independence. So the problem is much more than trust in the administration of a grant, but trust in the performance of academic duties. The simple solution I would like to propose is that managers should place more trust in academics, and reduce central control and the heavy administrative burden that it places on staff and the institution.

Of course I am not by any means the first to identify the problem—a quote from one of the papers referenced in the Managerialism section, reports on the results of a large survey of UK academic staff (Erickson 2020) and concludes that it reveals "*… an acute situation of endemic bullying and harassment, chronic overwork, high levels of mental health problems, general health and wellbeing problems, and catastrophically high levels of demoralisation and dissatisfaction…is a call to action to demonstrate, and support responses to, the woeful state of management and governance…academics cannot wait for university leaders to rise to a challenge they do not recognise…address this dilemma by developing a different way of thinking about accountability that restores trust and autonomy*".

Trust. Dirks and Ferrin (2001) tell us that "*Scholars from various time periods and a diversity of disciplines seem to agree that trust is highly beneficial to the functioning of organizations*".

Tallant and Donati (2020) use Mayer's definition '*Trust is the willingness to be vulnerable to the actions of another party based on the expectation that the other will perform a particular action important to the trustor, irrespective of the ability to monitor or control that other party*', and makes the point that "*Trust is a positive expectation regarding the behavior of somebody or something in a situation which entails risk to the trusting party.*" Das and Teng (2004) emphasise that trust does incur a risk and that there is a relation between trust and risk, with most definitions of trust implying risk.

Trust or control? The nexus between trust and control is complex—they are alternative organisational methods and as Bijlkisma-Frankema and Costa discuss (2005), "*…studies support the theoretical idea that trust lubricates relations between partners and organizational processes by promoting a variety of voluntary behaviours that enhance trust-building and performance.*" and "*the higher the level of trust in relationships, the lower the costs of monitoring and other control mechanisms*". Given this latter point about cost saving, it is surprising that universities have abandoned trust for control.

This is supported by a popular report relating to the business sector (2019) by Great Place to Work which summarises: "*There is a strong connection between a high-trust culture and business success. In fact, the connection is so strong that it can reasonably be argued that strategy-minded leaders, who care deeply about the financial well-being of their business, should make building a high-trust culture a top priority.*"

There are also suggestions that trust is important in the student teacher relationship (Houldsworth 2020), so an organisation which values trust between managers and

3.1 Develop Trust in Academic Staff to Replace Managerialism

staff might well find that this extends to improved educational outcomes among students.

The solution is clear—change the structure to increase trust in and independence of the academic staff. But is this warranted? Will there be threats to the quality of the education, research or service provision? Will there be benefits?

What about quality—is trust a risk for the quality of the educational product? On the contrary according to Dzimińska and colleagues (2018) who state that *"the intentional development of trust serves the purpose of enhancing the quality culture in higher education."*

Of course it works both ways, employees may have lost trust in their managers as well as the other way round. Brower and colleagues (2008) find that *"when they trust their subordinates, managers get employees who are more productive, extend help beyond the requirements of their jobs, and remain longer. Consequently, we can conclude that it is in the best interest of managers to trust their subordinates and to behave accordingly."* But also, there are mutual benefits when the employees have trust in their managers.

It needs to be said that the findings of a 2019 systematic review of the evidence (Guinot and Chiva 2019) suggests that the evidence of the benefit of 'vertical trust' is patchy.

Niekerk (2016) brings us back to the university sector and argues that *"the university during times of supercomplexity should focus on interrelationships between different sectors of the university to re-establish mutual trust relationships."*

So, there is a considerable amount of evidence that trust in employees increases productivity and job satisfaction. Why have universities globally reduced the trust in their staff and increased checks and controls? I suspect that this reflects outdated management theory, as well as an inappropriate risk management strategy. There clearly are risks to both the reputation of the institution and to the outcomes of student education and research excellence, if academics do not perform well and provide education of poor quality. There are reports of lazy tutors, researchers who cheat and falsify their results or plagiarise other peoples' work. But is increasing managerial oversight the best way to prevent this? Where are the evaluations that point to increased oversight as a risk management strategy in comparison with increasing the trust placed in the academic staff?

The Covid-19 pandemic has pushed more and more educational activity online. In other parts of this book, a massive scaling up of online education is one of the solutions I am suggesting for the higher education sector. Of relevance in this section is the increased transparency that this offers. All tutor/student interactions can be captured by the online platform software and are available for review. Course materials, discussion forums, examination marks and feedback are all there for the manager to explore in a way that is missing in face-to-face teaching. This has not been fully appreciated by university managers as a way of quality assessment, and requires less intrusion by central control mechanisms.

Another feature of the Covid-19 pandemic is a global and very fast drive to online teaching. This has depended critically on the skills and hard work of the frontline academic staff, with support from IT and educational designers, but the managers are much more remote and non-contributory in this process. So this has demonstrated the importance of trusting the academic staff without close managerial oversight.

A change of the power dynamic between academics and managers will introduce risk. It would be important to evaluate whether reducing the power of administrators vis a vis that of academics will lead to better outcomes, and actually facilitate or obstruct the main structural reforms which are required and discussed later.

Of course, it is possible that a reason that managers are not keen to move from managerialism to trust as their underlying strategy is that this would reduce their own relevance and result in job losses among managers. The cost savings for the institution would be considerable, especially if this is associated with a change from the corporatisation model and the high salaries to senior executives that this implies.

Since managerialism and the competitive business model are so intimately connected, a move away from managerialism will open up a number of other possibilities—starting with developing a focus on collaboration.

3.2 Focus on Collaboration—And a New Taxonomy

I previously described my experience of, and reservations about, the needless competition between universities for students and reputation. In this section I want to discuss the benefits of collaboration rather than competition. If the higher education sector were to take collaboration seriously, it would provide the potential to redress the mission of universities and tackle many of the problems I have identified. In this and subsequent sections, I outline some practical steps that could be taken by, within, and between universities.

We should start by adding collaboration as an important and measurable educational outcome as an attempt to change the culture within educational organisations. At its simplest level, preparing graduates to work as members of a team would seem to be an important way to ensure that a university education is relevant to the realities of the workplace, where teamwork is a key feature of most industries. If educational programmes within universities have elements of collaboration, this might sow the seeds for wider collaboration within and between universities. There is a great deal of evidence of the power of collaboration, and many excellent examples within the higher education sector, so what I am proposing is not a new concept.

I have been part of a number of research collaborations within and between universities, and one major educational collaboration—the International Clinical Epidemiology Network (INCLEN). INCLEN was a formative experience for me, only partly due to the fact that the grant brought me to live and work Australia. The Rockefeller Foundation funded three (and later four) universities in different countries to provide the educational components of a programme aimed at building capacity in what has come to be termed Evidence Based Medicine. Individuals from 26 universities in Africa, Asia, India and Latin America, from the disciplines of medicine, statistics, health economics and health social science were set up in multidisciplinary units on

3.2 Focus on Collaboration—And a New Taxonomy

their return from training. The units then performed collaborative research and developed their own educational programmes. From a small start in 1980, INCLEN (www.inclentrust.org) now comprises core functional units in 89 academic institutions in 34 countries.

The INCLEN programme demonstrated collaboration at three levels: between the education providers in three countries, between departments and disciplines within the educational programmes offered by these providers, and between the various academic disciplines in the units once established in the home universities. Although the programme and its results demonstrated to me the power of collaboration, it needed an external agency, the Rockefeller Foundation, to start and maintain it—for 21 years—before it achieved independence. As we consider the evidence for the power of collaboration, we can also think about the drivers and enablers of collaboration—there are not too many Rockefeller Foundations.

Kezar (2005) has documented some of the early research in this area, and I am using the quote to set the scene: "*…researchers have documented the benefits of organizational collaboration including greater efficiency, effectiveness, and perhaps most important for higher education institutions, it can enhance student learning. In addition, accreditors, foundations, business and industry and government agencies have been espousing the importance and value of collaboration for knowledge creation and research, for student learning and improved organizational functioning. As a result of both the external pressures and the known benefits, many forms of both internal and external collaboration have begun to emerge nationally. For example, in terms of external collaboration some campuses partner with local businesses to increase their teaching pool and internship potential and provide needed labs and materials for conducting research. An example of internal collaboration is the formation of cross-disciplinary learning communities that bring faculty and students together to study an issue, capitalizing on intellectual capacities throughout the institution for teaching. Similarly, faculty have begun to form multi and interdisciplinary research centers to address the pressing problems of our times and student and academic affairs divisions are working together to deliver joint programs and services.*"

In this section I go through the various types of collaboration that might be relevant.

1. To start—can we collaborate within an individual university?

You would think that this is easy, and that working with your colleagues towards a common good would be a high priority. There is even a substantial literature about how to collaborate effectively. There are some situations where it is essential for academics to work together, for example when a department wants to design a new course. However, collaboration is not always easy or fully understood by the academics: Newell and Bain (2020) have studied the perceptions of a group of academics engaged in course design about how prepared they were for collaboration. They report that "*The existing research also indicates that a complex matrix of personal, professional, social/cognitive and organisational factors are crucial to the effectiveness of team-based collaboration*" but that "*…participants reported that current conditions at the institutional level serve as inhibitors to collaboration in* *course design. This included the absence of committed leadership and organisational supports for collaboration. Participants described the dominant culture as more supportive of individualised, competitive and hierarchical work practices. Under these work conditions, participants noted a reliance on individuals' goodwill to collaborate in the absence of broader organisational structures and support....they did not express a depth of understanding about the cognitive and social capacities required for collaboration and the skills, structures and processes necessary to enable team-based collaborative practice".*

Collaboration in research is vital, as single person research is a rarity today with multiple skill sets required to tackle most problems. There are some rules that will make collaboration more productive, such as agreement in advance on authorship of resulting publications. Collaboration can be within or between departments and faculties, as well as broader as we discuss below.

For collaboration between departments, or faculties within the same university, the same issues apply, although threats to collaboration from competition for resources between departments are even more relevant than within departments.

But how to collaborate—what is needed?

Back to Kezar (2005) who describes a model for how institutions can move towards collaboration *"The first stage, building commitment, contains four contextual elements—values, external pressure, learning and networks. Here the institution uses ideas/information from a variety of sources to convince members of the campus of the need to conduct collaborative work. In the second stage, commitment, senior executives demonstrate support and re-examine the mission of the campus and leadership emerges within the network. The third phase is called sustaining and includes the development of structures, networks, and rewards to support the collaborations."*

There are a number of software tools to aid collaboration online, highly relevant to today's distributed world.

2. Can different universities collaboration with each other?

Mintz puts the need for collaboration very clearly (2019): *"The most striking consequence of institutional competitiveness is the failure of colleges and universities to focus on the needs of the ecosystem as a whole. Many of the most severe challenges facing colleges and universities can't be solved one institution at a time. Whether this involves improving enrollment of low-income and underrepresented students or increasing the number of non-traditional students who receive a meaningful degree, cross-institutional cooperation and collaboration, not competition, is part of the answer...The time has certainly come for a more collaborative higher education ecosystem with far greater sharing than is the case today."* He is calling for us to look at broader national needs for education, rather than just the needs of the individual university. This resonates with some of the points about national and global needs which I make elsewhere in this book.

There may be a number of ways in which funding bodies can promote collaboration between universities. However, there are also some structural barriers to collaboration between universities that could easily be overcome. An example of one of these is requirement by funding bodies in Australia to award the majority of the funds to a lead university, which can be a negative incentive.

I am pleased to say that there are some excellent examples of collaboration between universities. One example is the Biostatistics Collaboration of Australia http://www.bca.edu.au/ where six universities have combined to offer a master's programme. The collaboration was established to meet a national and international skills shortage and was the initiative of committed teachers. The programme has been going for many years and has an impressive list of alumni, as well as industry support as many industries need the skills that this programme produces in its graduates.

3. Can universities collaborate with other organisations?

My focus and experience has been in the health field, where 'industry' collaboration is fundamental and students are trained for professions in a very clear way. There is clear articulation between the education and the profession into which students graduate. In many countries, student numbers are restricted in order to populate, but not overpopulate, the profession—although predictions of numbers of doctors required are often incorrect and emergency catch-up and recruitment from overseas have been required in the past. Although the assertion that there were more Malawian doctors in Manchester than in Malawi appears to be a myth, the story of how the UK and Australia for example have populated up their own health workforce at the expense of the lower income countries is quite a disgrace. Health professionals emigrate to greener pastures, leaving the countries who trained them with ongoing manpower shortages. This is not, of course, restricted to the health professions.

Leaving aside the difficulties in predicting workforce requirements and the corrections that need to be made, health is one of the particular professions where universities can point to a clear relation between education and workforce needs. The marketplace for students does not in general relate closely to the requirements of the workplace. Universities can claim that a university degree teaches generic skills including how to learn and how to think critically, which will be important for any profession. And global workforce trends are difficult to predict. However, closer collaboration between universities and industry, to discuss needs and appropriate educational outcomes, should lead to less unemployment of graduates and more education that is fit for purpose. The Biostatistics collaboration discussed above is an excellent example. You will see that this is a key component of the distributed university structure that I propose in a later section.

More broadly Mehling and Kolleck (2019) suggest that collaboration across sectors and with practitioners is essential for the sustainability of the university sector. Unless the university sector takes this seriously, it may be left behind by other providers who link learning to industry needs—for example Google career certificates https://grow.google/certificates/.

4. What about international collaboration?

This can be between universities in any setting, and most, where they exist, have involved research collaborations among universities at similar levels of expertise and development. The European Union has a very strong record of facilitating research collaborations among European countries and beyond—the goals of its research and innovation policy are 'Open innovation, open science and open to the world are the 3 main policy goals for EU research and innovation.' https://ec.europa.eu/info/research-and-innovation/strategy_en Many universities across Europe have been part of research consortia, and have partnered with like-minded universities and research groups across countries.

The 'open to the world' policy is stated to be increasingly important, with one of the EU Commissioners stating: *"It is not sufficient to only support collaborative projects; we need to enable partnerships between regions and countries."* https://ec.europa.eu/research/iscp/index.cfm?pg=policy.

The EU also has a strategic framework for European cooperation in education and training, which emphasises collaboration between countries within and beyond Europe (https://ec.europa.eu/education/policies/international-cooperation/international-cooperation-and-policy-dialogue_en). There are many examples of international curricula and joint degrees.

This resonates with the Sustainable Development Goals, where goal 17, titled 'Partnerships for the goals', has the headline goal to 'Strengthen the means of implementation and revitalize the global partnership for sustainable development' (https://sustainabledevelopment.un.org/sdg17).

Rubin (2017) tells us that *"While many large universities collaborate internationally on research, very few have significant experience with intensive collaborative networking in pedagogy (the theory of teaching)"* and he reports on an international initiative, COIL, where *"teachers from two cultures work together to develop a shared syllabus, emphasising experiential and collaborative student learning."*

Joo and colleagues in 'Unlocking the power of collaboration' (2019) promote the value of higher education-focused networks *"Oriented around the cross-cutting problems of improving student success and social mobility, enacting structural and cultural change, and managing overlapping organizational responsibilities, these networks develop and strengthen enduring relationships that iteratively generate new ideas and processes to tackle the most pressing postsecondary problems of our times."*

The OECD report 'How international collaboration can help build the future of education' (2017) states: *"Collaboration is the key to finding solutions on complicated problems, and education is no exception. Through collaboration, people can build the collective intelligence necessary to address the world's complex problems. International collaboration enables countries and decision makers to connect and come together to learn from each other, find common answers and work for the common good."*

We will discuss the importance of online education in a later section, but in relation to collaboration, the OECD report (2017) identifies the key role that online learning has to play: *"Perhaps the most distinguishing feature of digital technologies is that they not only serve individual learners and educators, but can also build an ecosystem of learning predicated on collaboration. Technology can build communities of learners that make learning more collaborative, thereby enhancing*

3.2 Focus on Collaboration—And a New Taxonomy

goal orientation, motivation, persistence and the development of effective learning strategies".

5. If we need it, we'd better teach it and add collaboration as a core educational outcome

There is a strong literature about the benefits of collaborative learning, although I am not aware of any evidence for the carry-over of learning collaboratively to professional practice. There would seem to be a logic to hoping for both this carry-over, as well as the idea that if collaboration is a highly regarded educational outcome, the organisation that provides the education would be stimulated to practice collaboration in the way it organises itself.

Scager and colleagues tell us (2016) that *"Several decades of empirical research have demonstrated the positive relationship between collaborative learning and student achievement, effort, persistence, and motivation. Collaborative learning potentially promotes deep learning, in which students engage in high-quality social interaction, such as discussing contradictory information."*

Laal and Ghodsi (2012) define collaborative learning as *"an educational approach to teaching and learning that involves groups of learners working together to solve a problem, complete a task, or create a product"* and *"sets out major benefits of collaborative learning into four categories of; social, psychological, academic, and assessment benefits."*

If we are to teach collaboration, there need to be appropriate educational outcomes identified. Bloom's taxonomy has been in use for many years to help us define the outcomes we might expect at various levels of learning. Bloom devised his taxonomy of learning in 1956 and it was revised in 2001. In the pyramidal hierarchy, the 2001 version starts with 'remembering' and rises to 'creating' as the highest order skill. This classification has been very important in defining expected educational outcomes. For example, master's degrees might extend to the 'Analyse' and 'Evaluate' levels, and PhDs to 'Create'—the highest level.

Collaboration does not appear in either version, although a further revision to a 'digital taxonomy' did add collaboration as a separate element (Churches 2008). My suggestion is to add collaboration as a key component—and I have called this next version the 'New Bloom', as in the picture which shows each of the versions. I've put 'Collaborate' between 'Apply' and 'Analyse'—so it is a quite high level skill which will be needed at each of the levels above it (Fig. 3.1).

Building on the theme of collaboration and reduction in competition, the next section makes a suggestion for a university version of the International Baccalaureate which has been adopted in the secondary education (high school) sector.

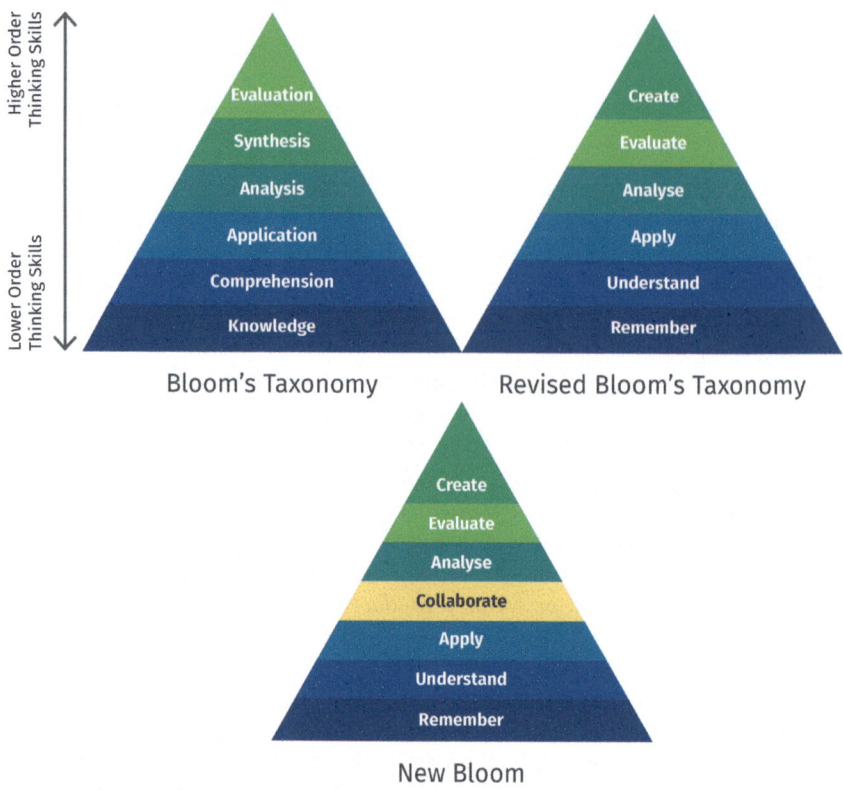

Fig. 3.1 The 'New Bloom' taxonomy includes collaborate

3.3 A Proposal for an 'International Baccalaureate' for Higher Education

Why does each university feel that they need to develop their own course? Why waste so much time, effort and resource? To reduce redundant duplication of the development of teaching programmes and competition between universities, I would like to suggest the creation of a higher education version of the International Baccalaureate used in schools. This would involve a global collaboration between universities that would reduce competition and standardise quality. Such an 'International baccalaureate' for higher education could be called the 'International Degree Programme' or 'International Tertiaire'.

An example from my personal experience is the Peoples-uni which offered online master's courses in Public Health for more than a decade, and to which I refer frequently. The course content is published under a Creative Commons licence, which means that anyone can use it provided they give appropriate attribution. The course has been designed and taught by an international faculty of academic and service volunteers who have considerable experience and expertise, and the programme has been reviewed favourably by an external evaluation. We have tried to offer the programme to universities who do not have such a course across a number of continents and countries—but without much success. Why does each institution feel the need to develop their own when you can have one ready made?

Although primary and secondary schools usually teach to a common curriculum, mandated by state or national bodies, universities have authority devolved to them to design and approve their own degrees within a general quality approval framework. In addition, there is a second framework that exists for some professional degrees which require national or international accreditation, to hold universities to account in those areas. There are attempts to standardise curricula, such as the European Bologna process (https://www.eua.eu/issues/10:bologna-process.html) which offers standards—what type of structure and length of study might you have in undergraduate or master's degrees for example. However, each university feels the need to develop their own degrees, partly to have some competitive advantage over other providers.

One of the major resource constraints of the higher education sector is the time and effort required to develop and 'manage' the curriculum and assessments. This not only uses academic time, but is used to self-justify the existence of a class of managers to oversee and provide quality assurance.

My suggestion is to offer, to those universities who want it, a standardised curriculum and course content. An extension could also offer the core educational process in addition to the content—the use of online learning could provide a common set of instructions, resources and feedback. The local university can add its own flavour in many ways, including the facilitation of discussions, timetable, input of local experiences, research supervision, and additional assessments. Most of the development and approval work, resources and managerial oversight can be 'outsourced' to an organising body. This would be another way in which savings could be made in managerial staff, academic time could be saved, common quality assured, and local expertise and variation accommodated.

The International Baccalaureate offers a potential model at the schools level, on which the Higher Education version could build. A common curriculum is offered, as well as a number of resources and offers of professional development for teachers. It mission statement (https://www.ibo.org/about-the-ib/) is:

- The International Baccalaureate aims to develop inquiring, knowledgeable and caring young people who help to create a better and more peaceful world through intercultural understanding and respect.
- To this end the organization works with schools, governments and international organizations to develop challenging programmes of international education and rigorous assessment.
- These programmes encourage students across the world to become active, compassionate and lifelong learners who understand that other people, with their differences, can also be right.

The term Baccalaureate actually means a bachelor's degree, the first level in higher education. So we would need a new term, such as 'International Tertiaire' (French for tertiary) or 'International Degree Programme', as well as some modifications of the International Baccalaureate structure to make it fit for higher education. I would hope that a philanthropic organisation might kick start it, but I think it would be sustainable through a small administration fee from participating universities in the manner of the International Baccalaureate. Since resources would be freely available to all, as described below, any participating university would be paying only for the accreditation and badging of their degree as part of the 'International Tertiaire'. This would imply a light touch online quality assurance process from the organisation to each participating university. The simplest mechanism would be an external examiner system with examiners from among the participating universities, and as a peer to peer assessment would provide benefit to both the examiner's home institution as well as the one under their external review. The whole programme could be mainly self-organised with groups of universities coming together around discipline groups. Of course an evaluation process should be built in from the start, and again this should be performed by the academics of participating universities with publication being the reward.

This idea would resonate with a number of the sections in this book—it would reduce unnecessary competition between universities, reduce opportunities for managerialism, enhance international collaboration and the internationalisation of education. The external examination and self-organisation into groups of universities each speak to the importance of inculcating trust, which is central to my suggestion to replace managerialism. All administrative and resource functions would be carried out online, and to resonate with the Plan E for education (in a later section of this book) with the curricula and resources being open source and becoming Open Educational Resources.

Once a philanthropic, or other, organisation has taken the bait to kick start this idea, various of the details will need to be discussed and revised before such a process would be piloted, evaluated, and subsequently introduced into practice.

Although the next section does not flow easily from the previous discussions on collaboration, it makes a suggestion to expand the current use of volunteer educators. This is not going to be a fundamental solution to the problems facing universities, but is generally ignored and can play a part to the benefit of volunteers, universities and students.

3.4 Utilise Volunteers as Untapped Educators

As a medical student, I learned the skills of clinical medicine from the doctors who were employed by the hospital rather than by the university. In those days, being on the staff of a teaching hospital was a marker of status—and probably allowed the doctors to charge higher fees in larger private practices—but the university did not have to pay the salaries. With some variation, this pattern for clinical skills teaching

3.4 Utilise Volunteers as Untapped Educators

provided by the profession, at least in addition to university paid staff, has continued and is seen globally. Most university courses that prepare students for any profession rely on similar expertise and commitment. It is vital that professionals help in the education of students destined for that profession so that the relevant skills can be learned.

Volunteerism is a part of many educational activities. Volunteer teachers work in schools and various professions offer work experience for schoolchildren. The Children's University Worldwide encourages people in the community to offer extra-curricular experience to children so that their education is broader than just that which they can gain at school. Many universities have volunteer programmes to add to the courses offered, such as language and acculturation programmes for students from overseas. Many countries encourage volunteer teaching in international settings—to the benefit of both the host country and the volunteers who go there and gain experience and satisfaction. The Granny Cloud http://thegrannycloud.org/ has volunteer *"native English speakers Skype in with children in these remote and disadvantaged locations and enable them to pick up English in the way we typically pick up any language—through hearing it spoken around us and using it in conversation"* The role of the 'Granny' is through online discussions *"providing praise and support to enable the children to work as a community and take the lead in their learning, helping them to explore and develop their natural curiosity"*.

My experience with Peoples-uni (http://peoples-uni.org) gives me the confidence to suggest that there is a great scope for increasing a role for volunteers in education. Peoples-uni relied on volunteers to provide all the educational tutoring and assessment activities in a master's level online capacity building programme. Over 14 years, more than 400 Public Health professionals, both on the academic and service sides, acted as tutors for students who are themselves health professionals and working in developing countries. There was a regular enrolment of volunteers, either having found the programme themselves or having been invited by a current volunteer. In any partnership, both partners need to gain something. So if volunteers provide a service, they need something back. Our Peoples-uni tutors gained personal satisfaction from helping others obtain skills which they can use for professional development and to help improve the health of their populations. But the tutors also gain practical benefits—they may be able to claim credit for this experience towards their own continuing professional development programme, they may learn both from the course materials and from the students about global health problems in different settings, they may learn about modern educational methods and information and communication technology, and they may be able to develop links and collaborations with other tutors and students for collaborative research. The benefits of collaboration, which we have previously discussed, maybe gained for use in the professional and personal lives of the volunteers. In a survey of Peoples-uni volunteers, *"The majority (75%) were keen to continue in their role for the foreseeable future and 71% felt very well looked after by their module leaders and colleagues. Responses highlighted that volunteers embraced the mission and characteristics of Peoples-uni."* (Heller et al. 2019a).

For professionals who work in a service setting, exposure as educators in a formal educational environment has extra appeal as a way of adding a dimension to their professional lives. This is the group which I suggest should be tapped in a more systematic way in the new sustainable higher educational future which I am postulating.

Volunteering is widespread, with rates of volunteering varying from 17 to 38% in different continents, although there are large variations between countries. There are socio-economic variations in rates of volunteering. Volunteers contribute the equivalent of many billions of dollars in employee wages. There is a scientific literature about volunteering, including a trend towards episodic volunteering rather than a constant commitment (Hyde et al. 2014; Southby et al. 2019) and there is evidence that volunteering may benefit mental health and survival (Jenkinson et al. 2013). Academics are used to volunteering their time as peer reviewers of journal articles and research grant applications.

Motivation to volunteer might be either altruism or self-interest (Nichols et al. 2019), although ideally it will be a mixture of the two. Doing something for others, while gaining benefit yourself, is a potent mix. The Peoples-uni experience shows that this can be achieved in an education programme—although we would not expect other educational organisations to be as fully dependent on volunteers.

So, there are many precedents and reasons for volunteers to contribute to education. We are missing many opportunities to capitalise on this and I suggest that our university of the future creates a systematic approach to the use of volunteers as teachers and support persons. As you see, this university of the future is online, enabling volunteer engagement irrespective of geography. There will have to be appropriate governance, including initiation and guidance, backup and the issuance of volunteer certification.

Here is how it may work. Both individual or institutional volunteering, where an industry offers its employees the opportunity, are encouraged. The university has a special volunteer section, with various support options for volunteers. These would include a centralised certification facility which departments can use to provide certificates for volunteers to recognise their service, resources to help volunteer teachers and support staff in their role especially on initiation, and news and forums to encourage a feeling of engagement with the institution. Volunteer options would be advertised and would include any and all of the functions of the university at all levels including leadership roles. The volunteer section should be staffed by those who understand the science of volunteering and who are prepared to contribute to it through evaluations which may be sent for publication. It would be important to automate most of the support functions and not turn the enterprise into another example of managerialism!

The next sections focus on the central importance I am placing on the use of online learning. It offers at least a partial solution to a number of the problems previously identified.

3.5 Move to Online Learning

Distance education has a long history, and the development of the internet has allowed this remote learning to move online. My first experience of developing a distance component was with INCLEN which I have mentioned previously. We found that some students who came to one of the training centres in Australia, Canada or the USA managed to find a way to remain and not return to their home countries. This reduced the impact of the programme which aimed to build local institutional capacity in developing countries. Creating a distance version of our course, where we sent materials by mail and visited for some tutorial activity, allowed us to continue to offer the education. We found we could scale up using this method to include more students as well as not depleting local manpower either during the course—or afterwards. We were able to transform the course to an online version as the internet became more available. My move to the University of Manchester allowed me to start a brand new fully online master's programme, and then to develop Peoples-uni on my retirement. My experience has made me increasingly enamoured by the concept and practice of online education.

My proposal is that the main mode of university education in the future will be through online learning. It will not preclude face-to-face experiences, and there are some things which can only be taught in person—learning brain surgery at a distance may not be sensible (although Virtual Reality and other IT developments may surprise us all in the future as technologic educational options). The question always asked is whether online learning is as good as face-to-face. My colleagues and I reviewed the literature (Heller et al. 2019b) and found that online learning was no worse than face-to-face, even better in some reports. This is consistent with other reviews (Cook et al. 2008) and (U.S. Department of Education 2009). The online format also has many educational advantages, such as the ability to encourage self-directed and active learning—and it does away with lectures! Actually, this is important—you cannot just put your lectures online and call it online learning, which requires its own specialised methodology. Online learning also allows a number of the other initiatives I canvass, such as increasing environmental sustainability and the ability to collaborate across universities and geographies. In the chapter on the case study of Peoples-uni, you will see that our fully online programme allowed us to have tutors from more than 50 countries to bring their expertise to the students. The future developments associated with the digital transformation of society, will only expand the opportunities and methods for the provision of online education. As the KPMG report The Future of Higher Education in a disruptive world (2020) states *"Spurred by the pandemic, but probably coming anyway, is the reverse situation. Courses will be designed to be delivered through technology—'digital first'—and supplemented by face-to-face, human support."*

The negative aspects of online education should not be dismissed. Many learners miss the social aspect of people meeting face-to-face and having para-discussions. There have been concerns expressed about the impact of the social isolation associated with online learning on mental health. However, it is easy to create an online community, and some people may actually find this better than the face-to-face experience. Adding the use of technology for education to all the other reasons that people go online could lead to fatigue associated with overuse, reduction in opportunities for exercise and other potential health effects. I am finding it difficult to obtain more than anecdotal evidence for most of this, but there are concerns. Again, these can be addressed through awareness and the design of methods to identify and mitigate potential overuse.

In addition, it is important to confront the issue of cheating, or plagiarism, in online education. There are conflicting reports of the prevalence of plagiarism at the university level—and whether much of this is actually cheating rather than a lack of understanding of how to quote and cite references (Kier 2019). There are a number of studies which find no difference in cheating between online and face-to-face teaching, as summarised by Pilgrim and Scanlon (2018). There are also excellent online software and other solutions that can detect whether something has been copied and pasted from somewhere else on the internet or by another student—these can also be used as an educational tool to help students avoid accidental plagiarism. There are also software tools to 'proctor' examinations to check that the right person is taking the examination online. Better than this, it is possible to tailor assessments in a way that requires students to report personal or contextual experiences that cannot be produced by someone else. These can be particularly useful at the higher end of Bloom's taxonomy of learning, and can incorporate the collaboration aspects which I have suggested be included in the New Bloom taxonomy. My personal view is that cheating actually cheats the students themselves—they end up without the skills and knowledge that they enrolled to gain. However, I do accept that education for a profession, whether this is online or face-to-face, does create an imperative to ensure appropriate knowledge and skills on graduation.

As discussed in a previous section, young people use the online space for so many of their activities, including learning both informally and at school. Failure to fully realise this in an educational context is misguided in the extreme, and misses a wonderful opportunity.

The next sections give more details on how to capitalise on this opportunity and make online learning central to university education, starting with a structure that will enhance environmental sustainability.

3.6 Place Education in a Framework of Environmental Sustainability—The Distributed University

As described in the 'Problems' chapter, there already are efforts to encourage environmental sustainability in higher education. These revolve around making university campuses more environmentally responsible, and educating students about the issues. There are an increasing number of initiatives to nudge universities in this direction, such as the student led People and Planet who have ranked UK universities according to their environmental and ethical performance (https://peopleandplanet.org/university-league). They use 14 indicators, from carbon reduction to ethical investment and banking. There are other lists of indicators, and toolkits to help universities make the transition—such as the Greening Universities Toolkit from the United Nations Environment Programme (https://www.unenvironment.org/resources/toolkits-manuals-and-guides/greening-universities-toolkit-v20). Others have their own lists of indicators, such as these five indicators: Energy (electrical and thermal energy); Water; Transport; Waste; Behaviour and management (Freidenfelds et al. 2018).

Many universities have excellent courses in environmental sciences including climate change, and some universities include climate change and environmental sustainability in each of their courses. These will raise awareness as well as developing leadership in tackling threats to sustainability.

However laudable each of these initiatives might be, all of these might be considered rather as tinkering than restructuring. If we are really serious about reducing emissions, universities will have to make much more drastic changes. Despite the global harm caused by the Covid-19 pandemic, the experience has pointed the way to such a restructuring. Students all over the world have found that they can learn perfectly well online. Tutors have found that they can offer rewarding educational experiences from their own homes. A serious pivot from face-to-face to online learning will reduce the impact on the environment from transport and through smaller campuses with fewer buildings. This is also consistent with a number of the other suggestions for change I am making in other sections, such as reflecting the way young people learn. The pivot to online education will also enable the transition from managerialism towards trust in academics as more direct responsibility flows away from central management.

Online learning needs little physical plant—so as we create the 'Distributed University' it will have a very different physical structure. The diagram demonstrates this new structure—and reflects three main components—teaching/research, administration, and the inputs from community, industry and national and global educational needs.

Physical action centres around local learning hubs where face-to-face opportunities can be provided. Teaching and research are provided through these local learning hubs which are distributed across geography and time, and are linked remotely to a central administration focus. Local networks of students around these local learning hubs would create self-directed and collaborative learning experiences, and include tutor support. They may have some physical space requirements for offices, face-to-face teaching or research labs, but where appropriate they might be virtual hubs with no physical plant. They should not become smaller versions of the central administrative focus. Some of the physical space requirements might be provided by local industry or community partners, who will also feed into local strategic development and provide educational experiences where appropriate for education for professions, and offer the opportunity for practice based education.

University administrations have reported a demand from students to resume the face-to-face contact from which they were deprived during the Covid-19 pandemic. This is understandable and probably largely reflects the social rather than the academic attractions of the university experience. Engagement by students with the local hubs proposed here will allow face-to-face contact as well as encouraging engagement with industry and community groups and practice based learning. A sense of belonging to a university community does not need face-to-face contact, and can be achieved though online activities including social media.

Local hubs will also provide the opportunity to engage with other educational providers, such as vocational and technical institutions. This will broaden the ability of the university to respect and respond to community needs, and may be easier to navigate at the local than regional or national levels.

All of these hubs would be supported by a central resource, housing central administrative functions and venues for occasional larger face-to-face meetings for staff and students. The central resource would be physically much smaller than the current university campus, using far fewer resources, and the reduction in managerialism would also lead to re-distribution of central administrative staff. Much of the central activity can be undertaken from home, as can many of the activities in other parts of this networked university. IT support and library facilities will themselves be online, and videoconferencing and online educational development teams would be critical educational infrastructure. This distributed structure will also facilitate educational networks between different universities nationally and globally (Fig. 3.2).

Relationships between the sections in the top half of the picture can be replicated in various local/global settings, and over time.

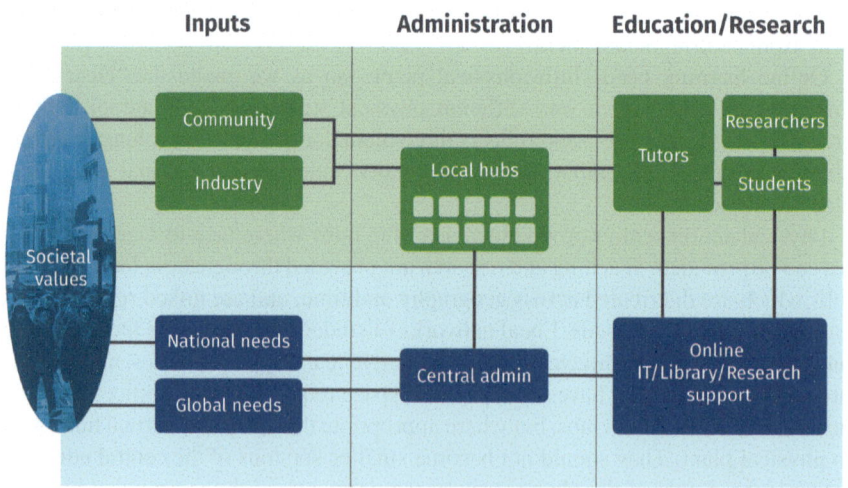

Fig. 3.2 The Distributed University

Online library and IT support, including educational design, are going to be key to the future functioning of universities. A grouping of these functions, which may or may not include a physical presence and which would also include research infrastructure, will support each of the local hubs and their students, teachers and researchers.

This model of the distributed university applies to place, as in the above diagram, and to time. The old model of university education taking place in the few years after leaving school has to be replaced by a system of learning appropriate to needs. There are learning needs at various stages of life, requiring lifelong learning.

This resonates with Alexander and Manolchev (2020) who envisage the university of the future *"combining high-levels of responsiveness (e.g. a digitally enabled model)… is the Interactive university"* or even a *"Platform university model…able to connect stakeholders in the process of life-long learning, mediating and participating in the co-creation of multi-disciplinary knowledge, as well as adapting to and catalysing change"*.

The term Distributed University has been used previously, by Haymes in a perceptive blog (2018) where he states *"The needs of knowledge creation have outstripped the physical and organizational infrastructures of universities (and, by extension, the business specializations that they have in turn created) more than ever before…We hope to create a professional organization with no physical "center" to leverage the connective tissue of the internet and united through a federative structure of ideas and principles."* There is also a World Distributed University (https://www.newportuniversity.eu/global-education-system/wdu/), although this mainly refers to a set of traditional university campuses across different geographical settings.

Stanford University has described the potential for the Open Loop University where students loop back to the university as their educational needs vary over time and they can learn what is applicable to them at a particular stage of their career (http://www.stanford2025.com/open-loop-university). Rather than 4 years after leaving school, they envisage 6 years over a lifetime. In the model of the Distributed University, these various components can be taken from different geographical settings, as well as at different times in the individual's life cycle.

Let me give a further theoretical approach to how learning needs will change over a lifetime, from the context of Public Health education. Colleagues and I (Madhok et al. 2018) have created the idea of a learning ladder where learning is a continuous process with different requirements at different stages of their careers (and of course afterwards) (Fig. 3.3).

The Learning Ladder describes how health professionals might progress through a career—their educational requirements will change as they progress. There are also, of course, learning needs that are not professionally related, to improve general literacy, knowledge and skills in many areas of leisure activity or to fit people to change career. With the projected increase in artificial intelligence and the reduction in jobs that this might replace, universities are in a great position to offer lifelong learning for these purposes. There is a need, once students have graduated, for continuing education to put theory into practice—distributing education over time as part of the new university structure I have proposed will fit in well if the university will take

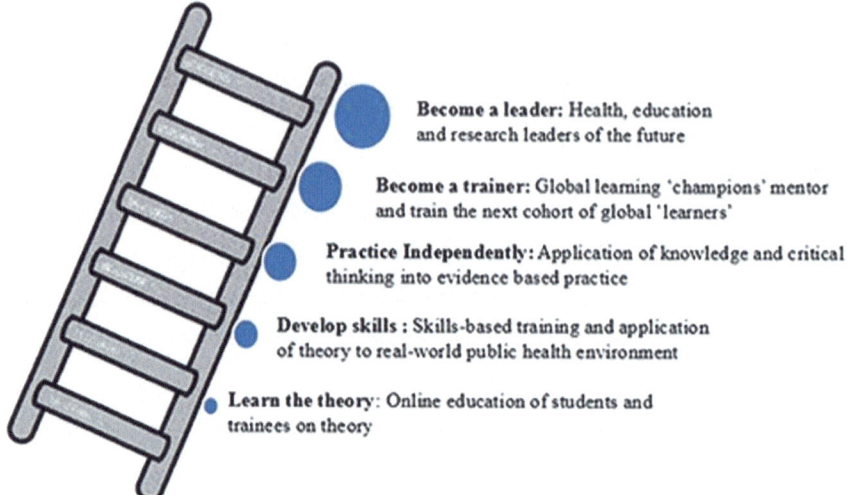

Fig. 3.3 The learning ladder

the opportunity to extend its responsibility in this way. There are other themes to this learning ladder, such as the sharing of experiences between low- and high-income countries in a global context—and we pick up this theme of global learning in a later section.

Central to the use of online learning will be the advantages that can come from using high quality educational resources that have been developed by others, and that are freely shared globally as Open Educational Resources.

3.7 Use Open Educational Resources

Open Educational Resources (OER) are '*teaching, learning or research materials that are in the public domain or released with intellectual property licenses that facilitate the free use, adaptation and distribution of resources*' (https://en.unesco.org/themes/ict-education/oer). The concept is logical and exciting—educators who develop resources share them with other educators—and in turn gain the reciprocal benefit of resources prepared by others. This avoids duplication of effort and has the potential for globally best practice resources to be utilised.

The idea has been extended to the term Open Educational Practices (OEP) which are the open context or environment in which the Open Educational Resources (OER) are used (Encyclopedia of Educational Philosophy and Theory 2020). OEPs ask how are OER best used in educational theory and practice, whether there is a mechanism for sharing and repositories where a teacher can go to access the resources, as well as whether universities have policies that allow or encourage the use of OER and if there are global agreements to facilitate the development and sharing of OER.

3.7 Use Open Educational Resources

This educational openness has arisen from the more general 'open source' movement which started with the sharing of code by software developers to improve and speed up the creation of computing solutions (https://opensource.com/resources/what-open-source). Each developer can build on the solutions proposed by the previous one, and their collective skills are more likely to achieve a useful outcome than can be achieved by any one individual. This movement, now much more broad than just for computer software, encourages collaboration and exchange of ideas and has the underlying notion of working together to meet a need rather than competition between the players to get there first. So you can see how this fits in with so many of the themes I have been trying to articulate in this book.

Open publishing of research findings has a similar notion, but is aimed at the user of the product, rather than the developer, although both may actually benefit. This is especially relevant for scientific publication. Why should scientific knowledge, especially if it has been created using public funding, be hidden from the readers who might benefit from it unless they can pay? The publishers say that someone needs to provide the funds required for the act of publishing, and of course this is true, but why should this involve profits for the publisher or their shareholders? An alternative way of meeting the costs of publishing is to ask the author to pay, and this is now a common form of scientific publication. A researcher will include publication costs of any journal article resulting from the research in a grant application, and pay the journal's publication fee. In return the article is published under a copyright license that allows free (online) access to any reader. Many government and other grant giving bodies now require that the publications from the research are in open access journals. Each of the research papers that we published about Peoples-uni was in an open access journal as a matter of principle—which is why as the author of this book I am paying the publisher's costs so that it can be freely available to anyone who wants to read it.

There are downsides to open publication of research. Two that have affected me personally are that research which is not funded by a grant requires the publication fees to be found elsewhere—difficult if your university department or the institution where you work is not well funded and even more difficult if you are retired! Of greater concern is the rise of predatory publishers. They make a profit by making a charge to unsuspecting researchers, and do publish the research in their online journal, but do not go through an appropriate peer review process. There is a lovely example (described by the author, Dan Baldassarre, on Twitter) of a journal article submitted as a sting, titled 'What's the deal with birds?' It was published less than a week after being submitted in a journal called Scientific Journal of Research and Reviews. The paper abstract (summary) was: "*Many people wonder: what's the deal with birds? This is a common query. Birds are pretty weird. I mean, they have feathers. WTF? Most other animals don't have feathers. To investigate this issue, I looked at some birds. I looked at a woodpecker, a parrot, and a penguin. They were all pretty weird! In conclusion, we may never know the deal with birds, but further study is warranted.*" In the acknowledgement section the authors said "*We thank Big Bird from Sesame Street for comments on the manuscript. Several trained monkeys transcribed videos."* The processing fees to authors by this journal vary from $649 to $1780, depending on the country of the author and the type of research article.

This journal and its publishers appear on various lists of bogus publishers, and researchers are advised to check these lists before deciding to submit to a journal. I personally had a recent experience of a different predatory journal where the chair of the Board of Editors was a respected academic with whom I had worked and published in the past. My co-authors and I submitted a paper for publication to the journal. Suspicions during the process were confirmed when we found the journal on a list of potential predatory publishers so we withdrew the paper—to be subsequently bombarded with requests for processing fees (which we did not pay). This attempt to charge withdrawal fees is common practice—as is the appointment of reputable people to the editorial boards who agree without appreciating the predatory nature of the journals. It is difficult to pick these predatory journals—my experience happened after a career which included the publication of around 400 papers in the peer reviewed scientific literature. In the end, the article in question was published in a highly respected journal, with an open review process.

Back to the topic of Open Educational Resources. There is evidence that the use of OER reduces student costs—mainly through access to free textbooks. There are also claims that OER improve learning outcomes (through access to these globally high quality resources). Most research studies of this actually find no difference in learning outcomes, but there are technical issues which might hide any demonstration of benefit (Grimaldi et al. 2019).

There is a great deal of international support for increasing the use of OER, with UNESCO taking a leading role. As recently as 2019, 193 countries voted to pass a UNESCO resolution (https://en.unesco.org/news/unesco-recommendation-open-educational-resources-oer). There are 5 action areas, which include international collaboration. A US based philanthropic organisation, the Hewlett Foundation was also instrumental in supporting OER developments, and there are a number of national initiatives such as OER Africa to push the notion. There is also an OER University (OERu) which offers free and open courses created by partner universities. In practice, however, there is not all that much take-up by universities. Peoples-uni developed a full master's programme with 18 modules, as well as a number of Open Online Courses for continuing professional development, using Open Education Resources and being made available to others through Creative Commons licences. In that way, we could select the best resources available internationally to use in our courses.

Nascimbeni and colleagues argue (2020) *"...that the use of OER can have an potential transformational impact on the way universities collaborate and work in increasingly complex and international contexts, mainly thanks to the collaborative knowledge building and the stakeholders' engagement dynamics that the use of OER can foster."* Despite the benefits, OER have not been adopted in any large measure by the academic community. Annand and Jensen told us in 2017 (2017) that *"OER are still not widely used, and progress toward large-scale adoption in most colleges and universities has been slow".*

I think that the main reason is that the concept is not compatible with the competitive underpinning of the current university business model. This competitive model has also been adopted by the academics themselves who feel they can design better material than anyone else! If universities are to become less competitive and adjust to the new realities of reduced funding and increasing adoption of online education, they do need to get serious about creating and using Open Educational Resources, and researching their appropriate place in education practice.

Online learning and Open Educational Resources take advantage of current communications technology, but looking to the future there are going to be a number of advances that will enhance the ability to transmit education between teachers and students. Some of these are discussed in the next section relating to the fourth industrial revolution.

3.8 Take Advantage of Modern Technology and the Fourth Industrial Revolution

I remember being appointed as a senior lecturer in the University of London, and finding that I had an office, with a full-time secretary at her own desk sitting outside my door. The secretary of course typed all my letters, and other duties included typing lecture notes and research articles. In an earlier job, a secretary typed up my doctoral thesis for me. Telling this to today's academic raises a laugh, as all these activities are now performed by academics themselves. While part of the reason to abandon such assistance to academics is financial, part of it is that the technology revolution that allows us to use computers, smartphones and other aids ourselves for these tasks. The use of computers characterised the third industrial revolution (the first industrial revolution was based on the discovery of steam and the second on electricity). The phases of the industrial revolutions have not mirrored the university generations which I discussed in the first chapter to any great extent, and today's third generation universities lag behind the third industrial, digital, revolution.

In a few years time, we will look back on the way we work now in amazement. There is another technology revolution occurring, the 'fourth industrial revolution' (4IR) which will change working and living practice, and the university sector will not be immune. Penprase (2018) describes the fourth industrial revolution as *"the result of an integration and compounding effects of multiple "exponential technologies," such as artificial intelligence (AI), biotechnologies and nanomaterials."* and suggests that *"More than ever, higher education in the 4IR age must develop the capacity not just for analyzing and breaking a technical or scientific problem into its constituent parts, but also must emphasize the interconnections between each scientific problem across global scales and interrelations between physical, chemical, biological and economic dimensions of a problem. The hallmark of the 4IR is exponential growth and rapid change, which gives the curriculum an imperative to update content on an unprecedented frequency to match the rapid tempo of scientific and technological advances."*

Barnett also warns us in 'Learning for an unknown future' (2012) that the super-complexity facing us in the future will have its own educational requirements that will need to be considered by universities.

I like this quote from the World Economic Forum website: *"The Fourth Industrial Revolution represents a fundamental change in the way we live, work and relate to one another. It is a new chapter in human development, enabled by extraordinary technology advances commensurate with those of the first, second and third industrial revolutions. These advances are merging the physical, digital and biological worlds in ways that create both huge promise and potential peril. The speed, breadth and depth of this revolution is forcing us to rethink how countries develop, how organisations create value and even what it means to be human. The Fourth Industrial Revolution is about more than just technology-driven change; it is an opportunity to help everyone, including leaders, policy-makers and people from all income groups and nations, to harness converging technologies in order to create an inclusive, human-centred future. The real opportunity is to look beyond technology, and find ways to give the greatest number of people the ability to positively impact their families, organisations and communities."* (https://www.weforum.org/focus/fourth-industrial-revolution).

The challenges of the fourth industrial revolution will require rapid change to be incorporated into educational programmes. Online education is going to be key to allow this to happen—and will in itself benefit from the associated technology such as AI. A new academic journal was founded in 2020, Computers & Education: Artificial Intelligence (https://www.journals.elsevier.com/computers-and-education-artificial-intelligence/) to report on explorations of the potential for AI to impact on education. We are going to have to make sure that AI can benefit the educational enterprise—for example in automating some processes to allow us to scale up in reach and numbers—rather than allow corporations to use captured big data for their own purposes to target advertising.

If universities are not able to respond to the challenge to help understand and harness these rapid developments, they will become increasingly remote from the needs of the population. Academics will be required to respond to and integrate the components of this industrial revolution, but currently are taken up with administrative duties that limit the time they can spend on these innovations.

Harnessing each of the themes discussed up to this point brings us to a key issue of special interest to me, that of developing a global perspective to educational needs. Next, I make some general points, and then make proposals for two new programmes—'Global Online Learning' and 'Plan E for Education'.

3.9 Develop a True Global Perspective to Reduce Global Inequalities in Access to, and Benefits of, Higher Education

While it is the responsibility of each nation to build its capacity of educated graduates, we have seen that there are gross global inequalities in access to higher education. Of course these cannot be tackled just by a focus on universities, as you have to be a school graduate in the first place to enter university and there are major inequities at this level as well. The Education Commission, a global initiative chaired by Gordon Brown, previously UK Prime Minister, and including various leaders in the fields of education, business, economics, development, health, and security, puts it well *"Education and skills are essential for the realization of individual potential, national economic growth, social development and the fostering of global citizenship. In the coming decades, as technology, demographic change and globalization reshape the world we live in, they will become ever more important."* (https://report.educationcommission.org/report/) The Commission feels that overcoming inequalities between countries is possible and calls for *"a Financing Compact between developing countries and the international community, realized through four education transformations—in performance, innovation, inclusion and finance."*

The suggestions I have are not as fundamental as those by the Education Commission, and only apply to universities, but in these next two sections I attempt to offer a way forward. Both suggestions that follow depend on online learning.

3.10 Reduce Reliance on Overseas Student Fees and Develop the 'Global Online Learning' Programme

Prior to the Covid-19 pandemic, there were warnings about the dangers of over reliance on income from overseas students. The KPMG report 'The future of higher education in a disruptive world' (KPMG 2020) stated: *"Those universities in low fertility rate jurisdictions which have hitched their business model to international students will urgently need to re-visit their strategy and reduce their costs"*. The Covid-19 pandemic exposed that in many countries the university sector was vulnerable to the financial risks from over-reliance on income from overseas students. At the time of writing, a number of Australian universities are facing bankruptcy and possible campus closure, and most are facing staff redundancies as the cash cow from overseas student fees dries up. The problem of this over reliance was well discussed before the event, although the part played by overseas students to the Australian economy was a source of pride by governments and the university sector. As a leader in the Economist says (The absent student 2020) in relation to the effects of Covid-19 *"Yet the disaster may have an upside. For many years government subsidies and booming demand have allowed universities to resist changes that could benefit both students and society. They may not be able to do so for much longer...Universities are rightly proud of their centuries-old traditions, but their ancient pedigrees have too often been used as an excuse for resisting change. If covid-19 shakes them out of their complacency, some good may yet come from this disaster.*" The Institute of Fiscal Studies estimates that UK universities may face a loss of a quarter of their income in a year as a result of the pandemic (Drayton and Waltman 2020).

As mentioned in a previous section, the ethics of using fees from overseas students to support national educational institutions in their education and research activities is highly questionable.

A year or so before Covid-19, I wrote a short piece with my suggestions for future-proofing in case of a reduction in overseas student numbers—I could not find a publisher and now it is not a case of future-proofing but of dealing with a current as well as future over reliance on overseas students. I will take it as read that, in line with other sections in the book, there is a wish among nations to improve global access to quality higher education. But can we do this in an ethical way with benefits to both provider and recipient nations, and that resonates with other suggestions I am making for a sustainable future for higher education?

The goal is to continue to offer educational opportunities to students from less developed countries until they are able to build local capacity, maintain the benefits to trade and cultural exchange with current and future 'target' countries, and reduce the reliance and consequences for both parties on overseas student fees. I will use the Australian setting, with which I am most familiar, and in essence suggest that this will be a low cost approach using online education and volunteers from the 'third sector', while continuing to provide the opportunity for students to travel physically for their education—but in fewer numbers. My suggestions about cost saving to help with a reduction in student fee income are in another chapter, but the development of a sustainable overseas student arrangement will also have long-term financial benefit, even if at a lower level than currently.

I have talked about the 'Learning Ladder' where educational opportunities are to be provided across the lifespan when needed to support various career stages. This came from a paper that my colleagues and I published titled 'Building public health capacity through online global learning'. In our paper (Madhok et al. 2018) we defined online Global Learning as "*innovative, integrated, global opportunities for capacity building through online learning and shared experiences between and within Low- to Middle-Income Countries and High-Income Countries, in a continuous process that helps health care workers learn as they progress through their careers*". It is from this title that I borrow the name of the programme I am proposing here—'Global Online Learning'.

This will rely first on online learning, often termed e-learning, as the delivery mechanism with a major contribution from the Third Sector ('*The Third Sector is constituted by all those organisations that are not-for-profit and non-government, together with the activities of volunteering and giving which sustain them.*'). The relevant features of online learning include: a wide reach across geographies, gender, levels of income and employment; costs of travel and accommodation are avoided, and manpower is not depleted during education; environmental sustainability; no evidence that e-learning is less effective than face-to-face teaching; and access to a wide range of educational resources that are freely available on the web (Open Educational Resources), reducing costs of production.

The Third Sector is often ignored in educational thinking, although there are many examples of education offered by volunteer organisations, where volunteer tutors provide benefit to both tutors and students. I have described the value of volunteers in a previous section, and they will be a key feature of the programme proposed here.

Here are some details of the programme—which in Australia might be called 'Australia Online'.

- Goal: to go beyond the nation's current educational offerings for overseas students to create low cost online learning opportunities which will not only help with current educational needs but provide a bridge to future and extensive mutually beneficial educational partnerships between Australia and emerging economies.
- Benefits: a boost to boost Australia's credentials as a provider of international education, while immediately offering valuable educational opportunities in countries whose higher education systems are less well developed.
- Programme to be a collaboration between the Higher Education and the Third sectors
- Design features: fully online; ensure that programmes meet needs of low- to middle-income countries in terms of the knowledge and skills learned and the capacities to be built.
- Oversight: programme sited in the Third Sector with a core staff, but needs input from Low- to Middle-Income Countries, the Higher Education sector, and accreditation to ensure relevance and appropriate standards.
- Funding: shared between governments, philanthropists, students and donations. Higher Education sector to offer access to some courses, staff time and accreditation.

Such a programme will not solve the problem of global inequalities in access to higher education, nor the over dependence on overseas student fees. However, if it works, it could be expanded and serve as a good model.

Next is another proposed programme that could help break down barriers to education globally, and builds on the Open Educational Resources movement.

3.11 Plan E for Education—Increasing Online Public Access to Higher Education

Although universities have to generate some of their own finances, and in many countries students pay at least a portion of the costs of their education, public money subsidises higher education in most countries as a public good. The figure below from the OECD report 'Spending on tertiary education' (OECD 2021) shows the

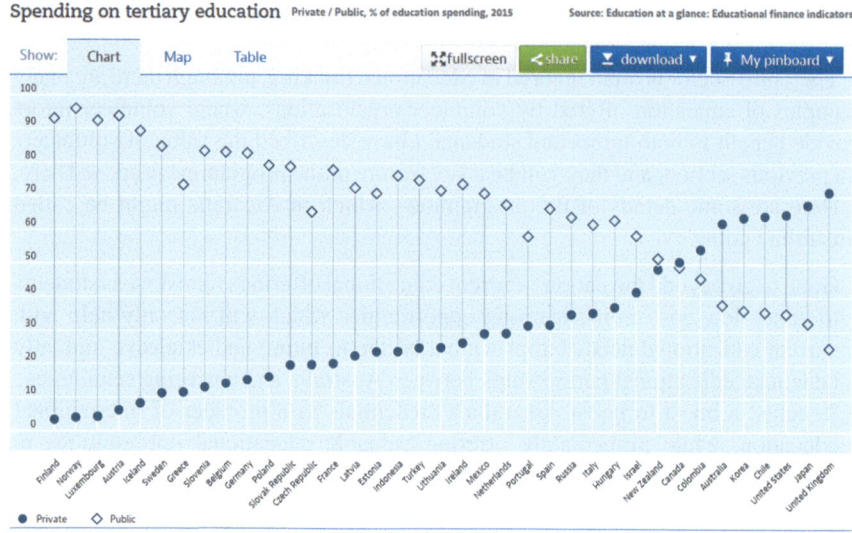

Fig. 3.4 Private/Public spending on tertiary education by country (OECD 2015)

variation among OECD countries, where in some countries the majority of funding is public money, and in others private funding contributes a larger proportion than from the public purse (Fig. 3.4).

The corporatisation of universities and the adoption of the competitive business model has resulted in higher education being sequestered behind massive 'paywalls'. Is it appropriate that public money should be spent on producing and delivering education that is not made freely available but is being used for competitive advantage by the universities that receive it? This discussion has been had over the years in relation to open publishing, and it is possible to use a Creative Commons licence https://creativecommons.org/ to publish your work so that it can be used by others (as in the case of this book). As discussed in the previous chapter on Open Educational Resources, a number of academic journals publish their articles using this kind of licence—and then the author, rather than the reader, has to pay the costs of producing and distributing the journal. I would like to offer a practical method to extend this concept from publication in journals and books, to educational materials produced by universities.

A good model on which to base this is Plan S, *"an initiative for Open Access publishing that was launched in September 2018. The plan is supported by cOAlition S, an international consortium of research funders. Plan S requires that, from 2021, scientific publications that result from research funded by public grants must be published in compliant Open Access journals or platforms"* (https://www.coalition-s.org/).

Although there have been some delays in the implementation of Plan S (https://www.nature.com/articles/d41586-019-01717-2), there is widespread global support for the notion that publicly funded research should be freely available and not hidden

3.11 Plan E for Education—Increasing Online Public Access to Higher Education

behind paywalls. There are already many examples of publications of public importance being made freely available—many of the early publications relating to the Covid-19 pandemic have been published as open access for the public good.

This proposal is to create something similar for higher education—'Plan E for Education' through open online access.

There are many examples of open access for higher education, such as the Open Educational Resources (OER) and the Massive Open Online Course (MOOC) movements. I have discussed the UNESCO recommendations from 2019 which encourages Member States to consider "*developing and implementing policies and/or regulatory frameworks which encourage that educational resources developed with public funds be openly licensed or dedicated to the public domain as appropriate, and allocating financial and human resources for the implementation and evaluation of policies*" (https://unesdoc.unesco.org/ark:/48223/pf0000370936). But how is this 'encouragement' going to lead to implementation? What are the measurable goals or targets, what is the timetable, is there going to be oversight and by whom, and are there financial needs and if so how are these to be provided?

Creative Commons has also established an Open Education Platform, "*a space for open education advocates and practitioners to identify, plan and coordinate multinational open education content, practices and policy activities*" (https://network.creativecommons.org/cc-open-education-platform/), and this has generated interest from educators in 78 countries.

There are also examples of universities putting their materials online for anyone to access—with MIT an early leader in the field, launching the OpenCourseWare initiative in 2002 with 50 of their courses published freely online, now extending to all their courses (https://ocw.mit.edu/about/milestones/). In my professional area, the Johns Hopkins School of Public Health has a wonderful set of its courses freely available online to others. I have thought, maybe unfairly, that the reason for this was a kind of advertising—you can get the resources, but need to enrol to get academic credit. I am pretty sure that this is the business model of the MOOC initiative where universities have spent large amounts of money developing free courses. Despite the promise of MOOCs, they are not taking over the educational world or meeting global capacity building needs—they are mainly undertaken by those in high income countries and those who already have a higher degree.

While there are differences between, and within, countries in their funding models for education, in many countries such as the USA, Canada, UK and Australia the business model of universities includes the charging of fees to students in addition to government funding. Access to educational materials by most universities globally is restricted to those who enrol as students, and universities compete amongst themselves for these students. This competition is partly for funding and partly for reputational purposes, as the higher education sector transitions from its primary function of public education to becoming business enterprises.

The idea behind Plan E is to question the rationale for educational resources, produced in whole or in part through government funding, playing into the competitive business model of the higher educational sector. Why are these publicly funded educational resources not be made freely available to those who might benefit?

There are examples of organisations who utilise open access educational materials making their higher education courses free or at low cost. These include Peoples-uni where volunteers translate available Open Educational Resources into programmes and courses for academic credit and continuing professional development (Heller et al. 2019a). These programmes aim to build capacity in low resource settings, where considerable benefit can be obtained by individuals and their communities through education which they would otherwise be unable to access.

Increasing access to high quality education materials produced by universities would allow their use both by individual autodidacts, as well as by organisations who would create other educational contexts for their use—such as Peoples-uni. Other organisations might also develop innovative delivery methods to contextualise open educational materials once such access was available. Thus high quality education, produced through public funding, can be democratised and spread where it is needed.

So Plan E would have three potential delivery strands—students access materials through the university that has produced them as per current practice, individual students could access materials for their own learning, and third party organisations can contextualise and deliver them in innovative ways.

In tandem with creating this access, we would suggest an accreditation system that would carry the accreditation afforded within the university who produced the material when it is offered outside the creating institution. This is more complex, but important for the originating university to be comfortable that the material is used appropriately. There could even be a staging post, where access is provided only to those who can provide an appropriate context for its use.

Asking myself the same questions that I used previously to criticise the UNESCO recommendation—the measurable goals or targets would be for all universities that receive public funding to make at least 10% of its offerings available online in this way within the next three years. The choice of materials would be up to the institution itself, but material of major global public interest should be prioritised. We would request that governments, state and national, as well as universities sign up to this. A philanthropic organisation would be identified to provide minimal infrastructure funding to allow an organisation, similar to cOALition S for science publication, to oversee the initiative, provide a repository or inventory of resources and consider accreditation. Could the Education Commission (https://educationcommission.org/about/) take up this challenge?

Having exhausted my suggestions for solutions, I need to explain how they can be afforded. This next chapter shows how most of these ideas are actually cost saving, and could help universities survive as well as innovate.

References

About the IB https://www.ibo.org/about-the-ib/

Alexander A, Manolchev C. The future of university or universities of the future: a paradox for uncertain times. Int J Educ Manag. 2020;34:1143–53. https://doi.org/10.1108/IJEM-01-2020-0018.

Annand D, Jensen T. Incentivizing the production and use of open educational resources in higher education institutions. IRRODL. 2017;18(4). https://doi.org/10.19173/irrodl.v18i4.3009

Barnett R. Learning for an unknown future. High Educ Res Dev. 2012;31(1):65–77. https://doi.org/10.1080/07294360.2012.642841.

Bijlsma-Frankema K, Costa AC. Understanding the trust-control Nexus. Int Sociol. 2005;20:259–82. https://doi.org/10.1177/0268580905055477.

Brower HH, Lester SW, Korsgaard A. A closer look at trust between managers and subordinates: understanding the effects of both trusting and being trusted on subordinate outcomes. J Manag. 2008;35:327–47. https://doi.org/10.1177/0149206307312511.

CC Open Access Platform https://network.creativecommons.org/cc-open-education-platform/

Churches A. Bloom's digital taxonomy. 2008.

Computers & Education: artificial intelligence https://www.journals.elsevier.com/computers-and-education-artificial-intelligence/

Cook DA, Levinson AJ, Garside S, Dupras DM, Erwin PJ, Montori VM. Internet-based learning in the health professions: a meta-analysis. JAMA. 2008;300(10):1181–96. https://doi.org/10.1001/jama.300.10.1181.

Das TK, Teng B-S. The risk-based view of trust: a conceptual framework. J Bus Psychol. 2004;19: 85–116. www.jstor.org/stable/25092888.

Dirks KT, Ferrin DL. The role of trust in organizational settings. Organ Sci. 2001;12:450–67. JSTOR. www.jstor.org/stable/3085982.

Drayton E, Waltman B. Will universities need a bailout to survive the COVID-19 crisis? Institute of fiscal studies. https://www.ifs.org.uk/publications/14919 (July 2020).

Dzimińska M, Fijałkowska J, Sułkowski Ł. Trust-based quality culture conceptual model for higher education institutions. Sustainability 2018;10:2599. https://doi.org/10.3390/su10082599.

Encyclopedia of educational philosophy and theory. Open Educational Practices (OEP) in higher education. July 2020. https://doi.org/10.1007/978-981-287-532-7_710-1.

Erickson M, Hanna P, Walker C. The UK higher education senior management survey: a statactivist response to managerialist governance. Stud High Educ. 2020.https://doi.org/10.1080/03075079.2020.1712693.

European Commission. Education and training: International cooperation and policy dialogue. https://ec.europa.eu/education/policies/international-cooperation/international-cooperation-and-policy-dialogue_en

Freidenfelds D, Kalnins SN, Gusca J. What does environmentally sustainable higher education institution mean? Energy Procedia. 2018;147:42–7.

Grimaldi PJ, Basu Mallick D, Waters AE, Baraniuk RG. Do open educational resources improve student learning? Implications of the access hypothesis. PLoS ONE. 2019;14(3):e0212508. https://doi.org/10.1371/journal.pone.0212508.

Guinot J, Chiva R. Vertical trust within organizations and performance: a systematic review. Hum Resour Manag Rev. 2019;18:196–227. https://doi.org/10.1177/1534484319842992.

Hastwell C. The business returns on a high-trust work culture. Great place to work. https://www.greatplacetowork.com/resources/blog/the-business-returns-on-a-high-trust-work-culture (2019).

Haymes T. Universitas Technologica: The Distributed University. Idea Spaces. https://ideaspaces.net/distributeduniversity/ (July 2018).

Heller R, Chilolo E, Elliott J, Johnson B, Lipman D, Ononeze V, Richards J. Do tutors make a difference in online learning? A comparative study in two open online courses. Open Praxis. 2019b;11:229–41. https://openpraxis.org/articles/10.5944/openpraxis.11.3.960/.

Heller RF, Strobl J, Madhok R. Online education for public health capacity building in low- to middle-income countries: the peoples-uni experience. IRRODL 2019a;20(1). http://www.irrodl.org/index.php/irrodl/article/view/3927

Houldsworth A. Trust me I'm a Doctor; The importance of trust in promoting high performance learning in medical education. MedEdPublish 2020; 9:184.

Hyde MK, Dunn J, Scuffham PA, Chambers SK. A systematic review of episodic volunteering in public health and other contexts. BMC Public Health. 2014;14:992. https://doi.org/10.1186/1471-2458-14-992.

Jenkinson CE, Dickens AP, Jones K, et al. Is volunteering a public health intervention? A systematic review and meta-analysis of the health and survival of volunteers. BMC Public Health. 2013;13:773. https://doi.org/10.1186/1471-2458-13-773.

Joo J, Sleingo J, Alamuddin R. Unlocking the power of collaboration. How to develop a successful collaborative network in and around higher education. Analysis and Policy Observatory. https://apo.org.au/node/264316 (Oct 2019).

Kezar A. Redesigning for collaboration within higher education institutions: an exploration into the developmental process. Res High Educ. 2005;46:831–60. https://doi.org/10.1007/s11162-004-6227-5.

Kier CA. Plagiarism intervention using a game-based tutorial in an online distance education course. J Acad Ethics. 2019;17:429–39. https://doi.org/10.1007/s10805-019-09340-6.

KPMG. The future of higher education in a disruptive world. https://assets.kpmg/content/dam/kpmg/xx/pdf/2020/10/future-of-higher-education.pdf (2020).

Laal M, Ghodsi SM. Benefits of collaborative learning. Procedia Soc Behav Sci. 2102;31:486–90

Madhok R, Frank E, Heller R. Building public health capacity through online global learning. Open Praxis. 2018;10:91–7. https://openpraxis.org/articles/10.5944/openpraxis.10.1.746/.

Making full and immediate Open Access a reality. https://www.coalition-s.org/

Mehling S, Kolleck N. Cross-sector collaboration in higher education institutions (HEIs): a critical analysis of an urban sustainability development program. Sustainability. 2019;11:4982. https://doi.org/10.3390/su11184982.

Mintz S. Creating a more collaborative higher education ecosystem. Inside higher Ed. https://www.insidehighered.com/blogs/higher-ed-gamma/creating-more-collaborative-higher-education-ecosystem (Jan 2019).

MIT OpenCourseWare. Milestones. https://ocw.mit.edu/about/milestones/

Nascimbeni F, Burgos D, Spina E, Simonette MJ. Patterns for higher education international cooperation fostered by Open Educational Resources. Innovations Educ Teaching Int. 2020. https://doi.org/10.1080/14703297.2020.1733045.

Nature News. Ambitious open-access Plan S delayed to let research community adapt. https://www.nature.com/articles/d41586-019-01717-2

Newell C, Bain A. Academics' perceptions of collaboration in higher education course design. High Educ Res Dev. 2020;39:748–63. https://doi.org/10.1080/07294360.2019.1690431.

Nichols G, Hogg E, Knight C, Storr R. Selling volunteering or developing volunteers? Approaches to promoting sports volunteering. Voluntary Sec Rev Int J Third Sec Res Policy Pract. 2019;10:3–18. https://doi.org/10.1332/204080519X15478200125132.

OECD. How international collaboration can help build the future of education. OECD 2017.

OECD. Spending on tertiary education. 2021 (data from 2015) https://data.oecd.org/eduresource/spending-on-tertiary-education.htm

Open educational resources. UNESCO 2017. https://en.unesco.org/themes/ict-education/oer

Open Loop University http://www.stanford2025.com/open-loop-university

Penprase BE. The fourth industrial revolution and higher education. In: Gleason N. (eds) Higher education in the era of the fourth industrial revolution. Palgrave Macmillan, Singapore, 2018. https://doi.org/10.1007/978-981-13-0194-0_9.

People and planet. How sustainable is your university? https://peopleandplanet.org/university-league

References

Pilgrim C, Scanlon C. Don't assume online students are more likely to cheat. The evidence is murky. The Conversation. https://theconversation.com/dont-assume-online-students-are-more-likely-to-cheat-the-evidence-is-murky-98936 (July 2018).

Rubin J. Collaborative Online International Learning (COIL). Internationalisation of Higher Education. 2017;2.

Scager K, Boonstra J, Peeters T, Vulperhorst J, Wiegant F. Collaborative learning in higher education: evoking positive interdependence. CBE Life Sci Educ. 2016;15:69. https://doi.org/10.1187/cbe.16-07-0219.

Southby K, South J, Bagnall A. A rapid review of barriers to volunteering for potentially disadvantaged groups and implications for health inequalities. Voluntas. 2019;30:907–20. https://doi.org/10.1007/s11266-019-00119-2.

Sustainable development goal 17. https://sustainabledevelopment.un.org/sdg17

Tallant J, Donati D. Trust: from the philosophical to the commercial. Philos Manage. 2020;19:3–19. https://doi.org/10.1007/s40926-019-00107-y.

The absent student. Covid-19 will be painful for universities, but also bring change They need to rethink how and what they teach. The Economist. https://www.economist.com/leaders/2020/08/08/covid-19-will-be-painful-for-universities-but-also-bring-change (Aug 2020).

The Bologna process https://www.eua.eu/issues/10:bologna-process.html

The Education Commission. https://educationcommission.org/about/

The international commission on financing global education opportunity. The learning generation—investing in education for a changing world. https://report.educationcommission.org/report/

U.S. Department of Education. Evaluation of Evidence-Based Practices in Online Learning: A Meta-Analysis and Review of Online Learning Studies. Washington, D.C.: Office of Planning, Evaluation, and Policy Development; 2009.

UN Environment program. Greening Universities Toolkit V2.0. https://www.unenvironment.org/resources/toolkits-manuals-and-guides/greening-universities-toolkit-v20

UNESCO General Conference. Draft Recommendation on Open Educational Resources. UNESCO 2019. https://unesdoc.unesco.org/ark:/48223/pf0000370936

UNESCO recommendation on Open Educational Resources (OER). https://en.unesco.org/news/unesco-recommendation-open-educational-resources-oer

van Niekerk P. The changing ethos of the university: living with supercomplexity. Acta Academia 2016;48:27–47. https://doi.org/10.18820/24150479/aa48i1.2.

What is open source? https://opensource.com/resources/what-open-source, https://Opensource.com

World Distributed University (WDU). https://www.newportuniversity.eu/global-education-system/wdu/

World Economic Forum. Fourth Industrial Revolution. https://www.weforum.org/focus/fourth-industrial-revolution

Open Access This chapter is licensed under the terms of the Creative Commons Attribution 4.0 International License (http://creativecommons.org/licenses/by/4.0/), which permits use, sharing, adaptation, distribution and reproduction in any medium or format, as long as you give appropriate credit to the original author(s) and the source, provide a link to the Creative Commons license and indicate if changes were made.

The images or other third party material in this chapter are included in the chapter's Creative Commons license, unless indicated otherwise in a credit line to the material. If material is not included in the chapter's Creative Commons license and your intended use is not permitted by statutory regulation or exceeds the permitted use, you will need to obtain permission directly from the copyright holder.

Chapter 4
But How Can We Afford It?

Abstract None of the issues and suggestions raised in this book are expensive, and most are cost saving.

Keywords Cost saving

4.1 Separating Teaching and Research Funds and Functions

I've already recounted my story of being introduced as someone who "breaks university rules but brings in lots of money so we don't mind". A small component of these funds came from external research grants, but the larger component was from externally funded education. Since those days, university funding here in Australia, and similarly in the UK and other countries, has been underpinned by fees from overseas students. We have discussed this before, but the issue has come into sharp focus at the time of the Covid-19 pandemic which has put a massive hole in university budgets, and affects research programmes. In Australia a considerable portion of research in universities is funded by the overseas student fees, either through the higher degree students who perform the research and bring their own funds, or through the revenue from the fee income which can support academic staff, laboratory and other costs.

This highlights the issue of the need to separate research and educational roles of the university. The core business of the 'higher education' system is…education. But if the funds from education are used to prop up research, what does that say about research as a national priority? There are anecdotal reports of university students getting very limited numbers of contact hours with any academic staff, and of students graduating without having been taught by a lecturer who is not either a higher degree student themselves or a contract teacher. The academic staff are drawn to research rather than teaching, as research grant success and research publications are the pathway to rewards in the university sector such as status within the organisation and promotion, although there are attempts to recognise teaching excellence. The various research excellence criteria used in some countries to guide university funding includes only research, not teaching, and most of the global university ranking systems are heavily research weighted. It is said that a high global ranking is required to attract overseas students (and their fees)—so we have a perfect circle of teaching funds being used to support research which attracts students who don't get teaching as a result of the funds they bring which are used to support research....

Not only is this not logical, it does not make business sense. I've criticised universities for adopting the businesses model, but what successful business would have a reward system that rewards non-core activities (research) more than its core business (education)?

While I have no problem with, and in fact would strongly encourage, research by university academics, I do not think that this should be at the expense of teaching. Research into teaching itself is essential so that the educational methods are evidence based. Similarly, all professional activities and public policies need research to ensure that they are evidence based. It is also important to fund 'blue skies' research. If research is a national priority, it should be properly funded, either within universities or in research institutes, and not as a spin off from teaching earnings. To use funds from overseas students, who will usually come from countries with a lower national income than the country where they go for their education, is particularly inappropriate, even unethical.

So my first answer to 'can we afford it' is—fund research appropriately and rather than siphoning off the funds earned from teaching into supporting research, use these funds for teaching.

4.2 Making Trust the Major Mechanism for Ensuring Quality

I've previously made the case for reducing the administrative structure and replacing it with a trust based model. Many universities, in accordance with their perceived notion that they are businesses, reward their senior administrators as though they were senior business executives with inflated salaries. In Australia, the administrative head of the university, the Vice-Chancellor, often earns more than a million dollars a year. The salary of the most senior academic is less than one fifth of this. Other senior administrative staff also have high salaries, so reducing the numbers of administrative staff will save a great deal of money. As will creating a more realistic salary structure.

And of course there are many other benefits of replacing managerialism with trust.

4.3 Changing the Educational Process

The consequences of a more sustainable process implies fewer buildings and more online education, and this will reduce costs. Fewer buildings and less travel are obviously going to save costs. There are some special cases of universities with multiple campuses where heavy travel costs are incurred just moving staff between

4.3 Changing the Educational Process

the campuses (usually professional staff and not academics). The divided opinion about the relative costs of online and face-to-face education is a false debate. Of course it takes more time and resources to develop a good online programme than to write some lecture notes, and if the lecture is given to 500 students and repeated regularly it will be pretty cheap. But if you want good quality education, the large lecture is not the way to go. We have discussed before that there is no reduction in educational outcome from the online format, even when the comparison is with good quality face-to-face education. Online education can be scaled up to large numbers, and as experience grows and infrastructure costs are spread over time, relative costs will reduce.

Getting serious about the use of Open Educational Resources and Practices will also reduce costs, along with the reduction in needless competition between universities.

In my notion of the Distributed University I have included links to local and national industries to make sure that education is relevant to needs. This will also have the consequence of deeper involvement through experiential opportunities and practice based learning, and these can be used to leverage funds as well as engaging the business partners as teachers—again with the implication of a reduction in university staff costs.

Beyond teachers identified as local industry partners, there are other ways of engaging volunteers in the educational process, as discussed in a previous chapter. This is a largely neglected opportunity to broaden the teaching staff, at low cost to the university.

I have not discussed how moving to a distributed model might be managed as this is beyond my expertise. However, change might be achieved through optimisation or by a transformation, depending on the level of ambition, the amount of disruption and the time over which this can be taken (KPMG 2020). There is considerable diversity in higher education, between countries who have different systems, between private and public, between arts and sciences and education for professions, and between undergraduate and postgraduate, teaching and research. The extent and pace of change in direction I have suggested will have to vary according to local realities, but should not be an excuse to avoid change.

In the final chapter, I present details of one of the global educational programmes with which I have been involved. This is to demonstrate a number of the issues I have discussed in other parts of this book, and has informed my thinking about university education.

Reference

KPMG. The future of higher education in a disruptive world; 2020. https://assets.kpmg/content/dam/kpmg/xx/pdf/2020/10/future-of-higher-education.pdf.

Open Access This chapter is licensed under the terms of the Creative Commons Attribution 4.0 International License (http://creativecommons.org/licenses/by/4.0/), which permits use, sharing, adaptation, distribution and reproduction in any medium or format, as long as you give appropriate credit to the original author(s) and the source, provide a link to the Creative Commons license and indicate if changes were made.

The images or other third party material in this chapter are included in the chapter's Creative Commons license, unless indicated otherwise in a credit line to the material. If material is not included in the chapter's Creative Commons license and your intended use is not permitted by statutory regulation or exceeds the permitted use, you will need to obtain permission directly from the copyright holder.

Chapter 5
A Case Study—Peoples-uni, and Conclusions

Abstract Peoples-uni was a volunteer led online programme to build public health capacity in low- to middle-income countries which demonstrated many of the features discussed as solutions. The term the 'Distributed University' is used to indicate the distribution of education to where it is needed—both reducing global inequalities in access and emphasising local relevance. It reduces impact on the environment, distributes trust in place of managerialism, and collaboration in place of competition. It distributes education online and sets up the higher education sector to adapt to the changes in the ways we work and learn today.

Keywords Distributed University · Sustainability · Peoples-uni · Volunteers · Public health · Low- to middle-income countries

5.1 Peoples-uni

When, in 2006, I retired from my post as Professor of Public Health at the University of Manchester in the UK, the School accountant doubled the fees for overseas students on the master's course I had developed. This was one the earliest fully online courses in the field of Public Health, and was aimed at building the capacity to develop and assess the evidence underpinning the ways we can improve population health. The need for this is much greater in low-resource settings where there are few numbers of skilled practitioners and educational opportunities. I had managed to keep course fees low for overseas students—you will have seen my previous comments about the ethics of charging high fees for overseas students. I channelled my annoyance at the fee increase by deciding to try to develop a low cost course for health professionals in developing countries: the Peoples-uni (official title People's Open Access Education Initiative http://peoples-uni.org).

The timing was good, as the internet was becoming more available globally, and the open source and Open Educational Resources initiatives were growing. A small group of colleagues and I put together the notion of a fully online programme, where we would create a number of course modules, each with a standard framework and populated by Open Educational Resources with a narrative to take students through these resources. Discussion forums to help students understand the concepts were to be run by volunteer tutors with relevant experience, who would also mark assignments. We held an initial meeting for those interested to join as tutors, and as the meeting room filled with academics and service professionals from all over the UK I realised that this could work (later on all our communications with tutors, students and support staff were fully online). We were then lucky to find wonderful IT experts with skills in educational technology platforms, who set up an open source platform for the programme and developed the supporting software. The Peoples-uni was born.

Registered as a UK charity, we developed a very flat and lean administrative structure with only one committee (to approve assignment results). Each of the 18 course modules had a leader who ensured that there are at least 5 tutors to guide the students through the semester, with each tutor only active for a two-week period in the semester. Although this was a master's level programme, anyone could enrol but entry to the master's course itself required students to pass at least two modules. This reduces the administrative load of viewing and checking students' previous educational and language certification, and ensures that those who enrol in a master's course have the language and learning capacity to achieve at this level. A small administrative fee was charged to the students, with a bursary scheme to waive or reduce even these low fees for those unable to pay. The online nature of the course modules allowed immediate changes to incorporate new resources identified during the discussions or course revisions. All activities were captured online providing is full transparency to allow internal quality control and external scrutiny of academic standards.

By the end 2020, more than 400 experts from 55 countries had been active tutors—each bringing their perspectives from their own academic or service experience, a truly international faculty. Students came from around 100 countries, 70% from Africa. More than 150 students graduated with a master's degree in Public Health, either through Peoples-uni or one of our university partners. Many more have sampled some of the modules. An external evaluation was very positive (Sridharan et al. 2018) as have been external examiner reports. Students have attributed promotions, new jobs and entry into PhD programmes to their experiences with Peoples-uni. Volunteer tutors also report positive experiences. You can read full details in this paper (Heller et al. 2019) or on the website http://peoples-uni.org.

We also developed another site for continuing professional development through free online courses on various aspects of global health, mostly developed by Peoples-uni but some hosted for others. There have been around 7000 enrolments from over 4000 students from more than 150 countries.

I have not met most of the tutors, or any of the students. We had no buildings or offices. All activities were online. One of our objectives to "*Work with the graduates of the educational programme, and other relevant partner organisations, in teaching, research, implementation of evidence-based health policy and advocacy to improve the health of their populations*" is realised through graduates being enrolled in an Alumni group who have performed collaborative research leading to publications, and a number of graduates have joined as tutors. We have published our experiences regularly and widely.

5.1 Peoples-uni

As testament to this success, Peoples-uni was the subject of a hostile takeover by a US led educational organisation in 2021. After 15 years, Peoples-uni closed down, but its work continues under new leadership.

Of course I am very proud of these achievements, but add this case study to illustrate some of the points in the book—many of which have been shaped by my experience with Peoples-uni.

- High trust in staff with absent managerialism
- Transparent processes and materials allow review and quality assurance
- Environmentally sustainable with no buildings or need for physical meetings
- Increase in availability of high quality education for those in developing countries to reduce global inequalities in access to education
- Responsive to needs and new resources
- Collaborative approach to course development and delivery, with university partners and with Alumni
- Tapping volunteer tutors who relish and gain from the experience.

I do not expect that this kind of education will totally replace the traditional university approach, as it is small in scale and cannot be generalised too broadly, but it does show that new approaches are feasible and sustainable. The scope of the book is broader than the experience of Peoples-uni provides, but the book is informed by this experience.

5.2 Conclusions

The start of the book identified a number of organisational problems, including managerialism, the adoption of the competitive business model and the downgrading of teaching in reward systems. Linked to these are the overdependence on overseas student income at the expense of tackling global inequalities in access to education, and the failure to foster collaboration or to respond to changes in the way people learn or the need for environmental sustainability.

Solutions include increasing trust and collaboration, and the creation of the Distributed University utilising open educational resources and online education underpinned by modern and future technology. Collaborative programmes for global education and increased access to open educational resources are proposed. A case study of a fully online global master's programme offers encouragement that at least some of these ideas are feasible, and finally there is reassurance that these solutions will save money.

The term the 'Distributed University' is used to indicate the distribution of education to where it is needed—both reducing global inequalities in access and emphasising local relevance in place of large centralised agglomerations. It massively reduces impact on the environment. It distributes trust in place of managerialism, and collaboration in place of competition. It distributes education online—which is the key to all of this and allows each of the above features. It sets up the higher education sector to adapt to the changes in the ways we work and learn today and which will be required to adapt to and take advantage of the fourth industrial revolution.

Many of the ideas, both the presentation of problems and the proposed solutions, may be painful for university managers to contemplate. However I really hope that those interested in the future of the higher education sector are open enough to take note of at least some of the ideas canvassed in this book. I also hope that the braver organisations will see the need to transform, and that governments and philanthropic organisations will sponsor the change needed. This would include the three new programmes which I have suggested: the 'International Tertiare (International Degree) Programme', the 'Global Online Learning Programme (Australia Online)' and 'Plan E for Education'. Each of these will complement the move towards the 'Distributed University' which will allow the higher education sector to have a sustainable future.

References

Heller RF, Strobl J, Madhok R. Online education for public health capacity building in low- to middle-income Countries: the peoples-uni experience. IRRODL. 2019;20(1). http://www.irrodl.org/index.php/irrodl/article/view/3927.

Sridharan S, Bondy M, Nakaima A, Heller RF. The potential of an online educational platform to contribute to achieving sustainable development goals: a mixed-methods evaluation of the Peoples-uni online platform. Health Res Policy Syst. 2018;16:106. https://doi.org/10.1186/s12961-018-0381-2.

Open Access This chapter is licensed under the terms of the Creative Commons Attribution 4.0 International License (http://creativecommons.org/licenses/by/4.0/), which permits use, sharing, adaptation, distribution and reproduction in any medium or format, as long as you give appropriate credit to the original author(s) and the source, provide a link to the Creative Commons license and indicate if changes were made.

The images or other third party material in this chapter are included in the chapter's Creative Commons license, unless indicated otherwise in a credit line to the material. If material is not included in the chapter's Creative Commons license and your intended use is not permitted by statutory regulation or exceeds the permitted use, you will need to obtain permission directly from the copyright holder.

The manufacturer's authorised representative in the EU is Springer Nature Customer Service Centre GmbH, Europaplatz 3, 69115 Heidelberg, Germany. If you have any concerns regarding our products, please contact ProductSafety@springernature.com

Printed and bound by CPI Group (UK) Ltd, Croydon, CR0 4YY
23/03/2026
02076446-0010